RADICALLY RESTORED

You know what I love so much about this extraordinary, life-altering, beautiful story? Even though it gives us an inside look at a man who has overcome unspeakable challenges to bring us joy and awesome music, it's not a Stephen McWhirter story. It's a Jesus story. My favorite. Read it and be changed.

—Dallas Jenkins, creator, *The Chosen*

Stephen McWhirter is a walking, talking, and singing miracle! Crushing disappointment and drug abuse almost destroyed him, but now he is a new person through Jesus Christ.

—Jim Cymbala, senior pastor,
The Brooklyn Tabernacle

I've known Stephen for about ten years and can truly say that his heart is what you hear when you listen to his incredible voice. I'm so excited that he is finally sharing the testimony behind such an incredible life and ministry.

—Matt Maher, Christian music artist

Do you know any "unlikely candidates" for the gospel—friends or family members who seem to be beyond the reach of God's grace? Or maybe the unlikely candidate is *you*? Take heart. God delights in reaching the seemingly unreachable. My friend Stephen McWhirter's story is proof: God can radically restore those in need of his amazing grace. Read this book to bolster your own faith. Then give it to others in your life who also need the radical redemption of Jesus.

—Mark Mittelberg, bestselling author,
Contagious Faith and *The Questions Christians Hope No One Will Ask (With Answers)*

God continues to use Stephen in a mighty way. His burning passion I've watched firsthand is to point people to Jesus and the mighty power of God that has changed his own life. You will be deeply touched by his story in *Radically Restored*. I couldn't recommend the book highly enough. Be sure to buy extra copies to give to friends who need to hear the message that no past is too dark for the grace of God to reach in and restore.

—Matt Brown, evangelist; author, *Truth Plus Love*; host, *The Matt Brown Show*; founder, Think Eternity

Stephen's powerful voice is matched only by the power of his testimony. His story will inspire you and remind you that God is writing a redemptive story with each of our lives.

—Matthew West, Christian music artist

RADICALLY RESTORED

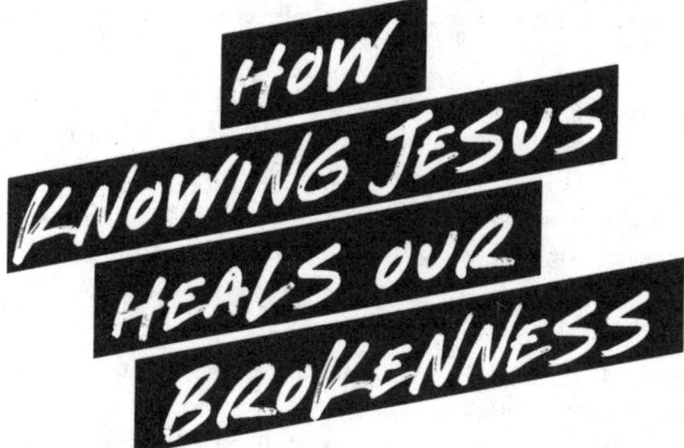

STEPHEN MCWHIRTER

ZONDERVAN BOOKS

Radically Restored

Published by Zondervan, 3950 Sparks Drive SE, Suite 101, Grand Rapids, MI 49546, USA. Zondervan is a registered trademark of The Zondervan Corporation, L.L.C., a wholly owned subsidiary of HarperCollins Christian Publishing, Inc.

Requests for information should be addressed to customercare@harpercollins.com.

Zondervan titles may be purchased in bulk for educational, business, fundraising, or sales promotional use. For information, please email SpecialMarkets@Zondervan.com.

ISBN 978-0-310-36953-0 (audio)

Library of Congress Cataloging-in-Publication Data
Names: McWhirter, Stephen, 1978- author
Title: Radically restored : how knowing Jesus heals our brokenness / Stephen McWhirter.
Description: Grand Rapids, Michigan : Zondervan Books, [2026]
Identifiers: LCCN 2025034134 (print) | LCCN 2025034135 (ebook) | ISBN 9780310369516 trade paperback | ISBN 9780310369523 ebook
Subjects: LCSH: McWhirter, Stephen, 1978- | Christian biography—United States | Ex-drug addicts—United States—Biography | LCGFT: Autobiographies
Classification: LCC BR1725.M3569 A3 2026 (print) | LCC BR1725.M3569 (ebook)
LC record available at https://lccn.loc.gov/2025034134
LC ebook record available at https://lccn.loc.gov/2025034135

Published in association with the literary agent Don Gates @ The Gates Group.

HarperCollins Publishers, Macken House, 39/40 Mayor Street Upper, Dublin 1, D01 C9W8, Ireland (https://www.harpercollins.com)

Cover design: Micah Kandros | Cover photo: Julia Weaver | Interior design: Kristina Juodenas

Printed in the United States of America

25 26 27 28 29 LBC 5 4 3 2 1

This book is dedicated to my mom, Ellen McWhirter. You are one of the kindest, most loving, and strongest people I've ever known. Thank you for never losing hope in prayer and believing for all God had in store for my life. I love you, Mom! Also, this book would never exist without my best friend and wife. Tara, I love you.

CONTENTS

FOREWORD

The most powerful stories are the ones that are true. And that includes the greatest story of all time: God's redemptive drama that played out through the life, ministry, atoning death, and resurrection of his unique son, Jesus Christ.

Because that account isn't based on legend or mythology but is historically supported, it means there is hope for all of us. And that includes such unlikely characters as me—and my friend Stephen McWhirter.

We both took circuitous routes toward faith. Mine wound its way through ardent atheism, petty ambition, endless bottles of booze, and a vain search for happiness in all the wrong places. And Stephen? Well, that's what this eye-opening and inspiring book is all about.

I'll let Stephen provide the details, which he does with admirable candor. But like many great stories, his has a surprise ending: a supernatural encounter with the God who graciously welcomed this rebellious character into his kingdom with open arms, just as he did for me years earlier.

Stephen's journey culminates in a vivid fulfillment of the apostle Paul's words in 2 Corinthians 5:17: "Therefore, if anyone is in Christ, the new creation has come: The old has gone, the new is here!"

I've seen this happen time and again. Cynical skeptics who are ambushed by God's truth and end up bending their knee to him. Jewish doubters who can't explain away the Old Testament prophecies that prove Jesus is the Messiah. Racists whose values and character are turned inside out by the gospel of grace. Muslims who were radically opposed to the biblical message but come to embrace Jesus as their Savior. Scientists, detectives, engineers, celebrities, homeless vagabonds, the wealthy, and the poor—their testimonies culminate in a divine encounter that left them transformed and heaven bound.

I can't get enough of these stories! They deepen my faith and stoke my desire to reach out to more and more people with God's triumphant message of hope and salvation, including those I'm tempted to think are beyond his reach.

I predict that Stephen's account of his own spiritual quest will inspire you in similar ways. In fact, I bet it will leave you cheering in the end. After all, what's more exhilarating than a real-life story of how God is patient and kind, forgiving and encouraging, gracious and loving, even toward the most spiritually lost and angry among us?

Today, Stephen and I share a common passion, one that we never would have foreseen in our earlier lives. We want to drag as many people to heaven with us as we can. That's why I hope that you will turn the page and accompany Stephen through the thorny pathways and unexpected twists of his spiritual adventure, and then give copies of this book to wayward friends and family members who need to know that there really is hope through Christ.

Even for unlikely characters like them.

—**LEE STROBEL,**
author of *The Case for Christ*
and *Seeing the Supernatural*

INTRODUCTION

YOU, FULLY ALIVE

I have come that they may have
life, and have it to the full.

—JOHN 10:10

I was alive, but dead.

I was in my early twenties before Jesus found me, moving from job to job, playing music in a band, but I was trapped—in the pain of my past, in hurts I couldn't leave behind, in unforgiveness that left blisters of bitterness inside, in addictions I couldn't find my way out of and, honestly, wasn't sure I wanted to. My life was full of darkness, without light or hope. But then Jesus came into it, and everything changed.

I'm not an expert on much or the smartest guy in the world. I mean, I can't do math without a calculator or write without spellcheck working overtime. But as the blind guy Jesus healed said, "One thing I do know. I was blind but now I see!" (John 9:25). Or the way I'd say it: I was dead, but now I'm alive. Meeting Jesus gave me life, and now there is nothing I care about more than knowing him and making him known.

You may not have a relationship with Jesus, and maybe you're not sure you ever could. Perhaps you can't even picture believing in him. But the emptiness you sense inside is like a dashboard warning light: You know something is off and you need help. If that's where you are, I understand. I was once there too. And I'm here to tell you, there is hope.

Or maybe you do believe in Jesus. Maybe you've given your life *to* him, but you don't feel like you're getting much life *from* him. He said he came to give abundant life, but that hasn't been your experience, at least not for a while.

In the 1987 classic movie *The Princess Bride*, an elderly healer named Miracle Max declares the hero, Westley, "mostly dead." You may relate. Your heart is beating, but you are missing out on life. You're afraid you'll be mostly dead until you breathe your last.

Wherever you are when it comes to believing in Jesus, I pray that as you read this book, you will start to believe you are made to be fully alive.

INTRODUCTION

NOT A BOOK BUT A HOPE

I believe Jesus is "the way and the truth and the life" (John 14:6), and I have experienced his transforming power and grace in a way that turned my life upside down. If God could grab me out of the depths of an abusive, dysfunctional family and a crystal-meth addiction to turn me into someone who truly knows and loves Jesus, leads people in worship all over the world, and has a happy, healthy family, he can do a radical work in your life too. You are not made to be the walking dead. You are made to be vibrantly, fully alive in Jesus.

In this world, you can easily find yourself just trying to get by. But you were made for more. You are loved beyond your wildest dreams. God is calling you out of the tomb. He is calling you to the fullness of life in him.

In the pages to come, I want you to meet the real you, the you God dreamed of before he created the sun, moon, and stars. In the Psalms, King David writes, "You saw me before I was born. Every day of my life was recorded in your book. Every moment was laid out before a single day had passed" (Ps. 139:16 NLT). God knows who he meant for you to be, the person he saw before you were even seeable.

Who is the *you* he created?

If you don't already know, that's something I can't wait for you to discover. Because you were made to be full of love without the grip of fear, full of hope without the depths of despair, fully free without the chains of addiction.

THE HURTS THAT HOLD US BACK

Do you know what you look like fully alive?

It seems like a question that would get a quick yes from everyone, but it's not always that easy. You may have been hurt so much you can't even begin to imagine what it looks like to be fully alive.

You may have family hurt in your past or continuing in your present. It could be that you're trying to stay away from it but it shows up every Thanksgiving.

It might be that you've experienced church hurt, where someone in the church wounded you. That person acted as a representation of Jesus to you and it left you uncertain about how to think of or embrace God.

Or it may be that you've hurt yourself. Your decisions have led you away from God and into pain. You've rejected him so much that you can't believe he could still love or want you. You've damaged yourself so much that you feel broken beyond repair. So this idea of becoming fully alive might seem like an impossibility for you.

I know what it is to feel too far gone, too lost in hurt and pain to believe anything good is possible. If you're in that place, I want to help. I'm not a fancy psychologist with a PhD, but I have a testimony to share. It's dark and contains dumpsters full of family trauma, hating Jesus, self-destruction, and addiction. I wasn't able to climb out on my own. But God, in his mercy, pulled me out. In the words of the psalmist,

> He lifted me out of the slimy pit,
> out of the mud and mire;
> he set my feet on a rock
> and gave me a firm place to stand.
> He put a new song in my mouth,
> a hymn of praise to our God.
>
> —Psalm 40:2–3

God can do the same for you! God can bring healing to your hurts so you can experience the life with him you were made for.

That is something you don't want to miss out on.

That is everything.

And that's what you can have now in this life.

One day, you will blink and this life will be over. And you'll be standing in the presence of Jesus. On that day, you will have zero doubt God is real. My guess is you'll stand there having thoughts like, *Why did I let my pride get in the way? Why did I let what someone did to me keep me from giving my heart to you, Lord? Why did I care what anyone else thought? You were always the deepest longing of my heart. Why did I ignore that?*

Don't wait. Jesus wants you to know him now.

YOUR HOPE AND FUTURE

Not one chapter of your life is meant to be wasted. Jesus can redeem every part, even what you think is beyond redemption. He can take what once branded your life with hurt or doubt or fear or shame and use it to mark your life with his glory. It may sound trite, but God's plan for your life is a million times more beautiful than anything you could ever imagine. He declares it: "'For I know the plans I have for you,' says the LORD. 'They are plans for good and not for disaster, to give you a future and a hope'" (Jer. 29:11 NLT).

I can tell you this promise is true because my story is living proof. God always keeps his word.

God has a plan for your life. It's time for you to live it out, to move into your kingdom destiny. It's time to move from mostly dead to fully alive!

CHAPTER 1

SON OF A PREACHER MAN

I tell you the truth, the Son can do nothing by himself. He does only what he sees the Father doing.

—JOHN 5:19 NLT

"Wake up!"

I was ten and my mother was bent over me, her voice a harsh whisper in my ear. It felt like she was screaming, but I could barely hear her.

I pried my sleepy eyes open. Even in the dark of night, I could see the panic on her face.

She helped me get moving by yanking off the covers,

grabbing my legs, and putting my feet on the floor. I slid into my shoes and grabbed my coat.

The next thing I knew, my older brother and younger sister and I were sneaking through the house and out to our car. We slid in and shut the doors as quietly as possible. My mom took a deep breath, started the car, put it in reverse, and sped out of the driveway.

No longer groggy, I had one thought: *Freedom.*

IT'S HERE

Years later, in my midthirties, I had a dream so overwhelming I haven't been able to shake it since.

I dreamed I was standing in a circle with my mother, siblings, and grandmother, praying in the living room of my childhood home. Suddenly, my sister shouted with terror, "It's here!" Like a scene from a horror movie, the door to my father's bedroom began to open slowly. Darkness emanated from the room. A paralyzing presence of fear pushed all of us to the ground. My family's faces began to distort and embody utter dread. To combat the dark presence, I was trying to speak the name of Jesus, but I couldn't even breathe enough to get the words out.

I abruptly awoke screaming, crying, and scaring my wife half to death. In that moment, I remembered what an eclipsing figure of trauma my father had been in my life.

SON OF A PREACHER MAN

I grew up the son of a traveling evangelist. Most of my childhood was spent in church camps all over the United States, where my father preached, primarily at weeklong revivals. I have some fond memories of those times. I made new friends at the different camps and enjoyed singing along with the hymns, at least early on. A few come to mind: "Victory in Jesus," "He Has Made Me Glad," and "How Great Thou Art." Those were some of the bright spots peeking through the dark shadows of my childhood.

My mom is a loving, beautiful, elegant woman. Though we didn't have much money, the way she carried herself could convince anyone we were high society. I remember her teaching my siblings and me fine-dining etiquette in the one-bedroom house where we lived as a family of five.

My wife, Tara, will tell you she was intimidated the first time she met my mom. We had just started dating. Tara was sixteen, and when she arrived at our house, my mother was operating a riding mower, wearing a formal dress, high heels, and pearls. My mom looked like she was riding the thing to church.

Mom is truly one of the kindest people you will ever meet. Sadly, underneath her elegant facade was a fearful need to give the appearance that everything was okay.

Our life was far from it.

My father and mother married young and really were in love. He was charming, well read, and could command a room with engaging stories and humor. He was the kind of guy whose preaching could lead thousands to come to Jesus. After a service, if you were walking into the restroom and he was walking out, he would tell you a tacky yet still somehow funny joke: "Tell 'em I sent you and they'll give you a good seat."

I wish that was the man I knew as my dad.

At some point in my parents' marriage, before I was born, a darkness started to manifest in my father. My mother told me about a day they were driving to a camp meeting and he got upset about something. He pulled over on the side of the interstate, opened the trunk, and began throwing her luggage onto the side of the road. This was one of her first glimpses of the broken man who would loom behind the curtain of our family for years to come.

As a child, I sat in many pews and watched people flood to the altar after my father's dynamic preaching. I have met people who tell me how God used my dad to bring them to Jesus and that he changed their lives. He was truly gifted. The Lord used him despite what you are about to read, because God loves those people who were saved under my father's preaching.

The man I grew up watching speak behind a pulpit was not the same man at home behind closed doors, where I had a front-row seat to the physical abuse he heaped on my mother.

In the late 1970s, before my birth, my father suffered back pain caused by obesity. When a doctor prescribed pain killers for relief, my father became addicted. The pain pills made it difficult for him to preach, so, trying to help, the doctor prescribed uppers. (Man, the eighties were crazy!) (Oh, who am I kidding? Right now is crazy too!)

Obviously, these drugs were a terrible combination for anyone, and especially someone I believe was already a narcissist and generally mentally unstable.

I can't recall the first time I witnessed the abuse. I was so young when he started hitting my mom that it seems he'd been doing it for as long as I can remember.

At about eight years old, I was playing in the living room with my sister when we heard screaming and a loud thud. We ran around the corner to see my mom falling down the stairs with a busted lip and blood on her face. My father ran down behind her, hitting her repeatedly.

Another time, I saw my father wrap a belt around my mother's neck and drag her across the hallway floor. I stood in the corner, screaming, "Stop, Daddy! Stop!"

I wanted to protect my mom, but I couldn't. There are no words for the helplessness I felt.

I spent most of my childhood nights in bed with a pillow over my ears to muffle the sounds of my mom screaming and crying as my father yelled and hit her. Though he never physically abused me or my siblings, he left us with too many emotional scars to count.

These are the kinds of things that never leave a person,

but if there is one thing I've learned over the years, it's that darkness cannot survive when dragged into the light.

HINDERED BY HURTS

The wounds of childhood are so powerful. We may want to pretend they don't affect us much, but we know that's not true. There's a reason why most counseling sessions end up drilling down into our relationship with our parents. So much of who we are and how we think about ourselves, about God and life, is formed in those early chapters of our stories.

Like me, you may have experienced childhood wounds in your family home, which should have been the safest place on earth. Those wounds can mark you in deep ways you may not even realize and can throw you off course.

If you had an abusive parent, you know what it's like to walk on eggshells for no reason, to always be afraid of what might happen next, to wonder why your parent was at their best out in the world but at their worst at home with the people they were supposed to love and protect. All of it has left you submerged in shame. Guilt is when you feel you *did* something wrong. Shame is when you feel you *are* something wrong. Perhaps that's how your parent made you feel, like there must be something wrong with you.

Or it might be that you had a negligent or absent parent.

Your parent didn't target you with hate, they just never showed you love. You yearned to feel affection or approval that was never there. Without it, you were left wondering if you were somehow incapable of being loved or if you had any worth at all. If your parents—who were obligated to love you—couldn't do it, who could?

Maybe you've experienced something so traumatic you've tried to block it out. The memories sit at the edge of your mind, ready to rush back when you feel weak or exposed. You've built walls around these painful experiences, hoping that ignoring them might make them disappear, but they still shape how you react to the world in ways you may not even notice.

Or perhaps after all you went through, you ended up hurting those you love. You became the monster in your story, and you feel unredeemable. Everything tells you that you should be cast out, never to return. Sometimes you even have trouble looking in the mirror.

Whatever you went through, your wounds can leave you feeling burdened and held back. They can keep you from becoming you, the real you, fully alive in Jesus. And the wounds are only complicated and intensified when the person who hurt you also professed faith in God. My dad claimed to embody Jesus while I watched him drag my mother through hell. How could someone like me love Jesus after living through such brutal hypocrisy?

Even if your parents weren't Christians, sociologists agree it's natural for us to assume that our heavenly Father is very much like our earthly fathers.[1] Even the best parents fall short. If your father was angry or distant, it's difficult to believe God is kind and close. We see the Father through the distorted lens of how we see our earthly fathers. As I write this, the Lord brings to mind this passage from John: "Jesus explained, 'I tell you the truth, the Son can do nothing by himself. He does only what he sees the Father doing. Whatever the Father does, the Son also does'" (John 5:19 NLT).

Everything Jesus did and said was birthed of his bond with the Father. This highlights how consequential the relationship is between parent and child. Jesus had a perfect Father, and it led him down the right path and into perfect life. Not all of us have a good father-child relationship, but Jesus shows us that with our heavenly Father, we can.

Our childhoods are crazy powerful, more than we care to admit. If yours, like mine, wasn't what it should have been, you may need to break free from your past.

I certainly did.

FLEEING FROM AND RETURNING TO THE PAIN

I had watched my father abuse my mother my entire life. As my mom rushed my siblings and me out to our 1980s Oldsmobile, I thought, *Is she really leaving him? Is this really happening?*

We had almost nothing with us, but we didn't care because we could all feel the weight of the moment. No one checks their pockets for car keys when being pulled from a burning building.

As we sped away into the darkness, an unfamiliar feeling washed over me. It was freedom. After years of choking on trauma, I could almost taste liberation. My young mind wasn't worried about how things would work out. My only thought was that we were escaping and might actually get to be happy.

We started our new life by staying with my mom's brother and his family. I remember pretending to play Ms. Pac-Man on my cousin's Atari as I eavesdropped on my mom's phone call to my father. I could faintly hear him crying and begging her to come home. Then, only twenty-four hours after our escape, we were all outraged when Mom told us she had agreed to return to him. I'm not sure why she decided to go back. Perhaps she believed his apologies were sincere or maybe she never planned to go all the way through with it in the first place; our leaving might have been a way she hoped she could get him to change.

I begged my mother not to go, to divorce him. I was confused and angry.

As I write this, my youngest son is ten, the same age I was the night we fled. I can't imagine him going through the heartbreak of having to beg one of his parents to leave the other, but that's exactly what I did. Yet there was no changing her mind. She was going back to him and taking us with her.

Going back into our home felt like returning to a crime scene, because that's exactly what it was. I could feel the darkness that loomed there.

My father set me and my siblings down on the carpet and promised he would never touch Mom again. It was so surreal. All I could feel inside was a mix of confusion, fear, and anger.

After we returned, my father eventually got off the pills and didn't touch my mom again. But to me he was still the enemy. There was no changing that. He could have begged that little boy for forgiveness a thousand times and I still would have hated him.

Ultimately, I couldn't separate my understanding of God from my disdain for my earthly father. I lumped it all together. After all I'd witnessed, I decided if God was real, he must not be good, and I definitely wanted nothing to do with this Jesus guy. All I saw when I looked at Christianity was my father, the villain of my story. I hated the whole thing and was determined to make sure the world knew it.

ATTACHED TO OUR PAIN

Have you noticed how easy it is to attach ourselves to our pain? It becomes a familiar blanket we keep ourselves wrapped up in. And if we live in hurt long enough, it can be hard to imagine our lives without it or nearly impossible to know who we really are apart from it.

When we've endured abuse or agony for a long time, even if we have a chance to get out, it can feel like the easiest thing to stay or go back. In some morbid way, we become attached to the pain.

Do you know about Stockholm syndrome? It's a psychological condition in which a hostage or victim becomes empathetic toward and even identifies with their captor or abuser. That's basically what happened to my mom. She took my father's side and gave excuse after excuse for his behavior. My mother believed the lie that there was no way out, and so her mind tried to justify how things were. She couldn't imagine her life without my dad, despite the pain.

She has told me many times that she was afraid that if people found out, it would undo all the good God had done through my dad's ministry. But if people are led to really know Jesus, rather than just knowing about him, through my father, a pastor, an author, or any other person, their faith would stay intact. If their faith is built on the foundation of knowing Jesus, it can't be shaken if those spiritual figures fall. Even so, if any of those people hurt us, especially a father or a husband, it's easy to feel trapped by the fear and hurt.

It may seem impossible to us, but Jesus wants to set us free from our pain. He said he came to set prisoners free, and though he was talking about freedom from sin, I believe that also applies to those of us who have been imprisoned by a lifetime of hurt. You are meant to live not from who you were but from what Jesus did for you on the cross. There is hope. Jesus promised that when he sets you free, "you will be free indeed" (John 8:36). He's not fooling around; the freedom he offers is the kind of freedom that breaks the chains so you never have to go back.

He wants to break the shackles that bind us to our past so we can walk with him into a new life.

> Are you tired? Worn out? Burned out on religion? Come to me. Get away with me and you'll recover your life. I'll show you how to take a real rest. Walk with me and work with me—watch how I do it. Learn the unforced rhythms of grace. I won't lay anything heavy or ill-fitting on you. Keep company with me and you'll learn to live freely and lightly.
>
> —Matthew 11:28–30 MSG

Jesus' words are for you, and I am convinced you are going to "recover your life" and learn to walk with Jesus "freely and lightly" in those "unforced rhythms of grace."

I promise you can be freed from your past and move forward into the kingdom destiny God has for you. If you find it hard to believe that right now, I understand. I wouldn't have believed it either when I was in the middle of my mess. It took me awhile. Before I got there, I went running in the opposite direction.

It got ugly fast.

CHAPTER 2

PRETEEN WASTELAND

For wide is the gate and broad is the road that leads to destruction, and many enter through it.

—MATTHEW 7:13

In my mind both my earthly and heavenly fathers were the villains in my story. The trauma of my childhood seared into me a rebellious spirit. I fell for lies and they led me down a path of self-destruction.

As I stepped into my preteen years, I was a wrecking ball of bad decisions. By the time I was eleven and twelve years old, I was smoking cigarettes, stealing things, and drinking alcohol.

I wish I could tell you that was all of it, but the darkest part of my story had just begun. Snippets of so many tragic moments remain as splinters in my mind. But those tragic moments are not where my journey ends. Rather, they are the things meant for harm that God ultimately turned around for good.

IN SMALL-TOWN HANDCUFFS

When I was growing up, my family lived in the small town of Corydon in southern Indiana. If you like nerdy facts, it was the first state capital of Indiana. It has one of those old downtown squares with a gazebo, like something out of an episode of *The Andy Griffith Show*—but only if Mayberry had secretly been a meth lab.

As a kid, I idolized my brother, Stuart. Yes, because he was older than me and seemed so cool, but more because one time I witnessed him stand up to our father. No one else would stand up to Dad, but Stuart did.

That night, my dad was going to spank me for something I did wrong. I don't remember what it was, but I might have deserved it. Back then we were whipped with yardsticks or an old-school leather belt. But that time, when Dad was about to swing, Stuart stormed into the room and yanked the belt out of his hands. My brother yelled at him and threw the belt to the ground. I didn't get whipped that night, and it made my brother bigger than life in my eyes.

In hindsight, I realize Stuart was just as wounded and angry as I was. He also lived through the nightmare of watching Dad's continuous physical abuse of Mom. He experienced it all while going through the turmoil of being a teenager. Those are hard years for almost everyone, but to witness Mom's suffering was terrible.

What's crazy is if you'd lived next door to us or visited our church and looked at my family, you would have been impressed. We seemed well put together and well behaved. You'd have had no idea of the nightmare we were all living inside our home. But no matter how hard any of us might try to cover them up, our sins and secrets have a way of seeping out for the world to see.

When I was eleven, I was caught shoplifting cigarettes at a Winn-Dixie grocery store. If you're unfamiliar with Winn-Dixie, just imagine a typical grocery store that screams "redneck." My crime fit the bill: I stole cheap, generic-brand cigarettes. I guess I was thinking, *It's Winn-Dixie, y'all. I can't take the good stuff!* So classy.

My mom was the one who came to get me. As she talked to the police, I could see the look of embarrassment on her face. She was obviously upset, but I don't recall having to deal with any real consequences. Perhaps with all my father put her through, she had become too familiar with drama.

I had all this anger inside of me—against my dad for the abuse, and against my mom for not leaving him. The trauma of all we'd gone through, mixed with the hormones of entering my teens, was like a Molotov cocktail of angst itching to explode. It kept pushing me to find boundaries my parents set so I could cross them.

When I was caught by the cops, I never thought, *Well, I won't do that again!* Rather, I convinced myself, *Ahh, I won't get caught again.*

Wrong.

Spoiler alert: Before turning twenty-one, I was arrested six more times—three for possession of narcotics and three for underage drinking. At one point, I was on probation in two different counties without either knowing about the other. Had they found out, I surely would have gone to a juvenile detention center and then prison. And there were many other times I should have been arrested, but somehow I outran the police through the woods or neighborhoods.

You'd think I would have learned, but I never did. It was like touching a hot stove and burning myself, only to turn around and do it all over again—and then again. It doesn't make sense, but looking back, I realize that's the deceptive nature of sin. No matter how often I hurt myself or others, I just kept coming back to it. I kept drinking poison, expecting different results.

At every opportunity, I rebelled and ran wildly down the wrong path. And not just in Corydon.

I LEARNED IT AT CHURCH CAMP

If you've been to church camp, you might know how much trouble you can find there. I guess it makes sense; many parents send their troubled children to these camps to find Jesus. Unfortunately, that's not always what happens.

Church camp in the early nineties is where I first smoked a joint and saw a *Playboy* magazine. It also had the pecking order of a prison yard. If I didn't prove myself to the other kids on day one, I'd be fighting for survival the rest of the week.

One year, I was sent home early from a church camp where my father was the guest preacher for the week. I was caught sneaking out of the boys' dorm after midnight and vandalizing the cafeteria. I was smoking pot with a few other kids behind the cafeteria and decided it would be funny to urinate in the water cooler. Just before going to the car that would take me home, I stole money and personal items from one of the dorms.

Today, I can't imagine being told my son was getting kicked out of a church camp where I was speaking and leading worship. But back then, I was so angry and lost.

My mom always shielded my dad from the reality of what was going on with us. I'm not sure he ever found out why I was sent home from camp, but my mother sure did. At that point, I think she was starting to get used to my destructive behavior. Honestly, this is just a glimpse of the unrelenting agony I eventually heaped on my parents and anyone else who dared have me in their lives.

ARRESTS, TRIALS, AND MY POOR MOTHER

In a small town like Corydon, every police officer knows who to watch. I was one of those people. A friend told me her probation officer, who was also my probation officer, was convinced I was the main supplier of meth and marijuana in our town. That wasn't true, but it wasn't a bad guess.

This may be part of why I was arrested so many times. One time when I was sixteen, the officer who pulled me over for running a stop sign also searched my car. Not normal police protocol for running a stop sign, but they searched my car every time. In all fairness, I don't blame them. I would have searched my car too. This time they found a small bag of marijuana stashed in my baseball cap, which I admit was a pretty stupid spot to hide it in. Of course, I'm not sure I've *ever* heard the phrase, "That pothead is a genius!"

I was put in handcuffs and, for the first time in my life, taken to the jail and placed in a holding cell. They took my fingerprints, and I thought, *It was only a matter of time.* When they told me I had one phone call, I immediately dialed my mom. With little to no finesse, I quickly explained the facts and asked her to come bail me out. Obviously shaken and emotional, she cried out, "Stephen! This can't be happening!"

As I've said, my mother is a kind, gentle, and proper lady. Her demeanor makes you wonder whether she might be a member of the royal family, but not in a way that comes across as aloof or rude. It's just her. That's the woman who entered the Harrison County Detention Center that night looking for her son. She looked at me through the bars with deep sorrow and embarrassment, tears running down her face. My mother had a way of letting us know she was upset, but with an "I still love you" undertone.

Getting arrested and hurting my mom should have given me pause, maybe even stopped me from continuing down the path I was on, but it didn't. I just kept going, regardless of who I hurt along the way.

I was arrested seven times. My poor mom would go with me from one court case to the next. My family didn't have much money, but she found a way to pay every bail, attorney, and court fee. She watched as some of my friends went to prison and others died. Today, many of the people I knew from those days have passed away, some even recently from overdoses.

I'm ashamed to admit I didn't feel as bad as I should have for heaping misery on my sweet mom. Deep down, it was hard for me to feel anything but anger. I think I actually wanted to be reprimanded by her. In my warped mind, her kindness and grace were the problem. I wonder if I believed those traits kept her from standing up to my father during all the years of abuse. That's terrible and not fair, but it was part of the war waging in my subconscious. At the same time, I also verbally assaulted her every time she did try to parent me. I think deep down I resented her for not leaving my father. After everything I'd watched her go through with my dad, I was being as abusive to her verbally as my dad was physically.

This may shock you: My mother swears she kept my years of addiction and arrests a secret from my dad. I know. How! My father had lived with a false persona for so long he perfected existing in denial. With the emotional tolerance of a toddler, he avoided everything, and we hid everything, afraid it would set him off. He may not have been physically abusive during my teenage years, but he still cast a shadow of fear over our home. Our unspoken family mantra was, "Don't let Dad know. He won't be able to handle it."

But I *wanted* my father to know what was going on. I wanted to get his attention. Most of my destructive behavior was my way of giving my dad a giant middle finger. I wanted him to see my broken life and hear me say, "*You* did this!"

Don't get me wrong, I know my actions were my own. At the same time, the mark a parent leaves on a child cannot be overstated.

I wanted my mom to tell him the truth so he would step

up and be a real dad, even though I knew there was no chance of that. I hate what I put my mom through, but I also hate that she had to go through it alone.

When I recently asked my mom what it was like for her during my years of addiction and arrests, she said, "I lived in constant anxiety wondering when I would get a call that you were no longer with us."

For all the pain I caused her, I believe it was her prayers that played a profound role in my ultimately coming to Jesus. If you have a prodigal, keep praying. Also, and I know it's not easy, don't carry the weight of their salvation; it's not all up to you. It's the Spirit of God who calls and convicts, and he won't stop chasing them with his love and grace.

My mother tells me how she and my grandmother would stay up praying for me when I was out all night. She says during that time she felt in tune with God. The Lord would weigh on her heart to pray for me right before something would happen. One time when I was eighteen, she was on a trip with my dad, who was preaching a revival, when she abruptly felt a need to jump on the first flight home. The very next evening, I was in a terrible car accident after a drunk driver pulled out in front of me. My femur bone was broken, and I was bleeding internally. They had to transport me by helicopter to the nearest major hospital for immediate surgery. My mom was the first person I saw in the hospital. She was always there even when I tried to push her away.

I didn't care how much pain I inflicted on those who loved me. And I also found ways to numb my pain.

BIKES AND BOOZE

When I was twelve, my bike meant freedom. My friends and I rode everywhere. Today, this is unthinkable for many parents. We are uncomfortable letting our kids leave the driveway without watching them. Back then, our parents wouldn't think twice about our riding all over town.

If you saw my friends and me, we may have looked like a group of innocent twelve-year-olds pedaling around Corydon. We weren't. If you smiled and waved, there's a good chance you would have received a middle finger and an expletive in return.

That was the year I started drinking. One day, a friend and I rode our bikes to a house, broke in, and stole some beer and a bottle of Seagram's Seven. That night ended as you might imagine, with my being so drunk I practically puked up my entire body weight.

Did I learn my lesson?

Nope. The next day, I was ready for round two.

One time we all rode our bikes to meet an older guy who drove a Ford Mustang and had agreed to get us alcohol. We scrounged our money together and he bought us a fifth of Jim

Beam whiskey. We were like something out of the Stephen King movie *Stand by Me*, only we were little rednecks.

Our town was all mobile homes and bonfires. I would often stay with a friend who lived with his grandpa. They had a small shack in the back yard where we spent nights getting drunk and smoking pot.

I never failed to follow my instincts and make the worst possible choices. My so-called friends would always be there cheering me on. I gravitated toward others who, like me, wanted either to push the boundaries or burn them to the ground.

IF IT'S NOT ALLOWED, YES

I had an unstoppable urge to pursue whatever seemed off limits. Everything I was allowed to do was boring, so I sought out whatever I wasn't allowed to do. I got more and more reckless.

When I was thirteen, I stole a car with my friend Nick. It was a giant brown 1980s Oldsmobile Cutlass Supreme with worn-out shocks, which made it feel more like a boat than a car. I tried to turn this brown behemoth around in the middle of some old country road and obliterated a mailbox. Whoops. Nick and I decided to return the car to where we found it, with a new dent I'm sure would always be a mystery to the owner.

The ironic part of that fiasco is that Nick went on to

pursue a career in law enforcement. Years later, when I was arrested for possession of an illegal narcotic and placed in a jail cell for a night, Nick turned out to be the jailer. He served me breakfast and asked if I was going to be okay. I shook my head. "Probably not, Nick." He could tell I was in a dark place.

Nick went on to become the sheriff of Corydon, Indiana. Today, he is a follower of Christ. I have performed and preached at many worship nights in my hometown since giving my life to Jesus, and Nick always brings the inmates. Many of them end up giving their lives to Jesus. God is using Nick in a powerful way.

THE PROWLING LION WHO LIES

Thinking back on my preteen days—especially on those days I rode my bike to meet people who would buy me alcohol, or to spend the night getting high in my friend's backyard shack—I wonder, Why did my parents let me go? They had to know what I was doing. Why didn't they stop me or at least say something? There were a few times when my mom tried, but I'd blow up and she'd quickly give up and let me go.

A fear of confrontation looms in some families. As parents, children, or siblings, we're afraid that acknowledging an issue might get us labeled as disloyal or lead to rejection. Or we fear what we'll have to deal with—conflict or abuse—if we address it. It's difficult, but when someone we love is headed down a wrong road, we need to have enough love to confront them and then work toward healing what is wounded.

It's tragic that I had no one telling me to stop making self-destructive choices. I had almost zero guidance in my life. My mother would tell me, "Stephen, make good choices," but I wouldn't listen. Ultimately, there was no one I could look up to as a positive role model.

I was totally alone, which is ironic because I was always with a friend or even a group of them. But have you noticed how you can be surrounded by people and still be isolated? You can hide in a crowd, pretending everything is fine when you know it's not. You won't share what's going on or ask for help, even though you need it.

All of this is exactly what the enemy wants. The apostle Peter warns us, "Watch out for your great enemy, the devil. He prowls around like a roaring lion, looking for someone to devour" (1 Peter 5:8 NLT). A lion hides in the tall grass, stalking a group of gazelles, waiting for one to wander away from the others. The lion then attacks the lone gazelle.

That is exactly Satan's strategy. He wants us isolated and vulnerable so he can attack. How?

With lies.

In the beginning, Satan, in the guise of a serpent, led Adam and Eve to fall away from God's purpose for their lives by getting them to believe a lie.

> One day he asked the woman, "Did God really say you must not eat the fruit from any of the trees in the garden?"
>
> "Of course we may eat fruit from the trees in the garden," the woman replied. "It's only the fruit from the tree in the middle of the garden that we are not allowed to eat. God said, 'You must not eat it or even touch it; if you do, you will die.'"
>
> "You won't die!" the serpent replied to the woman. "God knows that your eyes will be opened as soon as you eat it, and you will be like God, knowing both good and evil."
>
> The woman was convinced.
>
> —Genesis 3:1–6 NLT

You probably know the rest of the story. Adam and Eve believed the lie, ate the fruit, and fell from God's original design.

Why? Satan, whom Jesus described as "a liar and the father of lies" (John 8:44), deceived Adam and Eve into thinking God was not trustworthy. That story of deception isn't in the Bible just because it happened once; it's in the Bible because it still happens.

It's exactly what happened in my story. Satan pounced on the opportunity given him by my father's hypocrisy and convinced me that it wasn't just my father who wasn't good; my heavenly Father wasn't good either.

Satan uses deception to keep us from God and the life he has for us.

THE TRUTH WILL SET YOU FREE FROM THE FEEDBACK LOOP

The antidote for a lie is truth, but the problem is we often don't speak truth to ourselves. God cautions us that "the heart is deceitful above all things" (Jer. 17:9). We lie to ourselves, convincing ourselves God isn't good and is holding out on us. Our deceived hearts begin to believe that what we're doing isn't sin, or that we don't have a problem, we're different, and we can stop anytime we want.

Have you ever been to a concert and heard a feedback loop? It's that ear-piercing squeal that occurs when sound going into a microphone comes through a speaker and then goes back into the microphone again. The sound frequency just keeps looping and looping, which causes that horrible sound.

That's a pretty good analogy of what happens when we isolate ourselves. When we believe lies and speak them to ourselves, the lies keep circulating like a feedback loop. Lies come in, go out, and come back again, reinforcing the deception. Without someone to speak truth into our lives, we get stuck in the loop.

You are not made to go it alone. You are meant to be a dwelling place for the presence of God and to live in community with others.

Go back and read the previous paragraph again just so it sinks in.

You're meant to live with God and others because it thwarts Satan. He is terrified that you'll kill your feedback loop of lies by abiding in Christ, living in his Word, and being in community with other believers. What he's most afraid of is your finding out the truth of who you are made to be in Jesus. If you believe that truth, the kingdom of God will advance through your life. For the enemy, that's a big problem.

But that's exactly what you need.

Jesus said he is the truth (John 14:6) and that he came so "you will know the truth, and the truth will set you free" (John 8:32). The gospel is freedom. The first step to be set free from the lies you believe is to give your life to Jesus so you can know and live in his truth.

You will not make it without Jesus, and you need people in your life who know him. Take it from me. Without that, I ran wild down a road of over-the-top rebellion and self-destruction. Jesus said, "For wide is the gate and broad is the road that leads to destruction, and many enter through it" (Matt. 7:13). I had a lot of room to act like an idiot. Note that Jesus said "*many* enter through it." I had so many friends doing drugs and acting crazy I decided it must not be that big of a deal.

I want to encourage you to do whatever it takes to draw close to Jesus and to get some people in your life who love him—and who love you enough to speak truth to you.

When you open yourself to the truth, your life will change. You will start to see who you really are in Jesus—the you fully alive—when you "let God transform you into a new person by changing the way you think" (Rom. 12:2 NLT). Remember, the root of bad decisions and all of the damage they cause is believing lies about who God is and who you are. You need to replace those lies with his truth.

If, like I did, you believe the lie that God is not good, you can start by replacing it with the truth: "You are good and do only good" (Ps. 119:68 NLT). Ask God to show you the truth, and surround yourself with some faithful friends who will remind you of it when you forget.

Replace the lies with God's truth.

If that sounds simple, it is. God is not trying to make it hard for you to know him; that's what the enemy is trying to do. The devil is constantly putting up obstacles to keep you from the truth of who God is and the life God wants you to live. Scripture is where you find the truth that can set you free.

Sanctification is a big old fancy-sounding churchy word, but its meaning is pretty awesome. To be sanctified means to become more and more like Jesus. And that includes becoming fully alive.

How does that happen? Jesus prayed for us, "Sanctify them by the truth; your word is truth" (John 17:17).

If we don't stay connected with Jesus and with others who know him, we will continue to live in lies and keep going down wrong paths.

Unfortunately, that's exactly what happened with me.

CHAPTER 3

IF IT'S BROKE, KEEP BREAKING IT

I could ask the darkness to hide me
and the light around me to become night—
but even in darkness I cannot hide from you.

—PSALM 139:11–12 NLT

Have you ever owned something you deeply loved? Perhaps it was something you saved up for to finally purchase, or a family heirloom handed down from one generation to the next.

Not too long ago, my wife and I bought a new Ford Escape. It wasn't anything flashy, but it was a big deal to us. We went on and on about how we were going to take care of it and keep it like new. I annoyed my family by not letting them eat in the car or leave anything in it.

I was the new-family-car police.

Four days after purchasing our new vehicle, I drove it to pick up carryout from a nearby restaurant. (Yes, that meant food would be in the car, but it was okay because I was taking it home. I wasn't going to eat in the car like an animal.) I parked in a spot that had concrete posts on the driver's side. *Perfect, no one can park next to me and ding my car when they open their door.* I remember being a little too excited about picking up the delicious food. I hurried back to my shiny, spotless car and quickly backed out of the parking spot. That's when I heard it. To this day, I vividly recall the crunching sound of steel and aluminum on the front driver's side. Yes, I had turned our brand-new car into the concrete post to my left.

I felt like an idiot, which is not that big of a surprise. Here's what did surprise me: I immediately stopped caring so much about the car.

When it was perfect, I wanted to keep it that way; but now that it was damaged goods, I felt like, *Who cares about the car now that it's damaged?* The kids want to bring their fries and ketchup in the car? "Go ahead, it's already a mess." You want to start a bonfire in the car? "Might as well."

I went from accountable to apathetic in a flash.

Looking back, I realize that's how I once felt about my life. After I started sinning and piling up bad choices and addictions, I thought I was too far gone to ever come back, so I might as well keep going. I saw myself as damaged goods that didn't matter anymore.

I wonder if a lot of us do this. We sin and then decide there's no point in turning back, so we just keep pouring gasoline on the fire. We fall for the lie, "If I've gone this far, what's the point in turning around?"

Do you know the saying, "If it ain't broke, don't fix it"? For many of us, it's more like, "If it's broke, keep breaking it!"

Basically, I lived my life by that mantra.

By the time I was sixteen, I'd tried LSD, pills, cocaine, and just about every drug under the sun. The only exception was needles because I was so squeamish I could never bring myself to inject something into my body. But that didn't stop me from snorting, smoking, or ingesting any narcotic I could get my hands on.

Was I trying to fill a void? Fit in? Or was I under the delusion I could be happy only when I was high?

I think maybe all of the above.

One thing I know for sure, I was going for broke and no one was going to stop me.

Purple Jesus

My brother, Stuart, is eight years older than me and was my only real role model. When I was a kid, I saw the movie *The*

Lost Boys. My brother reminded me of the character Michael, played by Jason Patric, who was the cool older brother to Corey Haim's character, Sam. Today, my brother will tell you he wasn't a great example to follow. I wanted to do whatever I saw him do. The first time I smoked a cigarette was because I found his hidden stash.

At one point, Stuart lived with friends in a house in Louisville, Kentucky, which is only a forty-five-minute drive from Corydon. When I got my driver's license, I often drove over to hang out with him. Back then Stuart had long hair and typically wore a leather jacket and sunglasses. He looked like a member of a nineties rock band. And just like the stories I'd heard of rock stars, he and his friends drank and did drugs most nights. I thought they were the coolest people on the planet. I'm not blaming my brother for my own mistakes, but the truth is I would do whatever I saw him do. I just wanted to be like him.

I was fifteen the first time I took LSD with two of Stuart's friends. He wasn't there, but they welcomed me nonetheless because I brought the drugs. Ironically, the acid we took was called Purple Jesus. After taking it, one of them drove us to his parents' house in middle-of-nowhere Indiana. During the ride, I started to hallucinate from the acid. Keep in mind this was my first time. The dusk-to-dawn lights streamed before my eyes, exploding with color like fireworks. My brother's friend was driving what felt like a hundred miles an hour down a narrow country back road. He was blaring the classical piece "Ride of the Valkyries" over and over, laughing hysterically. I felt like I was in a twisted version of the helicopter scene from the movie *Apocalypse Now.*

When we arrived at his parents' home, he took me into the basement, where we watched *The Shining*, a horror movie that makes you feel like you're on acid even when sober. Yes, I was having a hard time keeping it together.

The whole night was traumatizing for me, but even still, I thought it was cool that I had taken acid with my older brother's friends. Really, though, we were just broken people breaking things together.

The last time I took acid, the person with me thought it would be funny to tell me I couldn't remember how to breathe. If you know anything about hallucinogens, you're probably aware how fast reality can slip away. In that moment, I truly believed I didn't know how to breathe. Just like that, I stopped breathing and passed out. I nearly had a total mental break.

Though I quit LSD, I didn't stop walking down my path of self-destruction. Soon I was staying up almost every night snorting cocaine, drinking alcohol, smoking pot, and finally taking painkillers to get to sleep. On several occasions, I almost killed myself with this ridiculous and dangerous combination of uppers and downers. Somehow, each night I survived, and I would get up and do it all over again the next day.

You have to admit, I was persistent.

METH OR DEATH

When I was seventeen, someone introduced me to a drug called crystal meth. Since the age of eleven, my story had been a drug-induced downward spiral, but this was a new low.

Crystal meth is an upper. You can snort it, shoot it up with a needle, or smoke it. I chose to smoke it. I placed a rock of meth on a piece of aluminum foil and burned it with a lighter underneath the foil. When the smoke rose up, I inhaled it with a small straight glass pipe between my teeth. Not a pretty picture, I know.

The effect? Instant euphoria and excitement.

The first time I used it, I knew I was in love and would need to have it every day for the rest of my life. Starting the next morning, I woke up every day immediately focused on where and how I was going to get more.

When you come down from meth, you're buried by an unbearable wave of depression and emotional instability. Probably the most destructive aspect is how it makes you believe you can never be truly whole without it. That's likely true with most addictions, but something about meth imprisoned me more than other drugs.

On meth, I became even more conversational than I am naturally, which means I talked so much I could open a portal to another dimension. I thought it made me more creative. I wrote so many songs on meth that were utter trash, but I believed they were masterpieces. (They were pieces alright. Ha!)

During this time, I somehow got a pretty decent job working for a media duplication company doing graphic design and DVD and VHS duplication (which I know dates me). Throughout the workday, I frequently sneaked off to the bathroom to smoke meth. When I came back, there must have been an obvious change in my personality. It wouldn't have taken much sleuthing to figure out I was on something. But I was under the impression it made me the fastest and best employee on the planet. Ultimately, I was fired. I was confused and devastated. Why would they fire me? Yeah, meth doesn't make you the smartest person in the world.

Growing up, I saw movies with addicts desperate for their next score. I always wondered how pathetic someone must be to let themselves end up like that. I never in a million years imagined I would become that person in real life.

One time, after being awake for four days straight on crystal meth, I sat in my car watching the sun come up and realized I would die at a young age from this addiction. The really scary part is that I was okay with it. The idea of quitting the life I had chosen was out of the question. For me, there was no fork in the road, only a grave to fall into. It may seem inconceivable to prefer death over sobriety, but that was my reality.

Looking back on my years of crystal-meth addiction, it

feels like an out-of-body experience. How could I have made such monumentally destructive choices?

It seemed I always ended up in the darkest situations. I will never forget sitting in the living room of a typical suburban family's home when I was about eighteen. Someone had told us there was a party at this house, so we went. This was not some graffitied, rundown crack house. At first glance, it looked like the home of a doctor and his family. A bunch of teens were drinking in the garage. We sneaked into the house, where the parents were enjoying the party. I watched as the parents verbally and physically fought with their teenage daughter over their next hit of meth. It was next-level evil. I could actually feel darkness wrapping itself around me. It was choking any hope of life out of me.

I even knew someone who had been cooking meth and blew up their trailer with their infant child inside. They both died. It was heartbreaking.

Did that deter me? No.

Have you heard someone say, "I can stop anytime I want. I just don't want to"? Well, I didn't want to change, but I also felt like I couldn't, even if I wanted to. I had fallen so far. I was too broken. I couldn't remember what it felt like to be happy without taking something to give me that feeling.

I had created an entire life around my trauma, my hurt, my anger and addiction.

BLAME AND COMPLACENCY

I was really good at breaking things, which makes sense because I was so broken myself.

It seems like I came into every situation asking, "How can I burn this to the ground? How can I make the worst choices possible?" If I wasn't inflicting trauma on myself and others through addiction, I did so through my anger. I may not have been physically abusive with anyone, but my rage and depression were volatile. I put my fist through many car radios and walls.

Interestingly, I don't remember thinking of myself as broken. I've found that's often true. Instead of thinking of ourselves as broken, we point and blame.

We blame our circumstances: "It's not my fault I did this. Anyone would have done what I did in the same situation. Why do these things always happen to me but no one else?"

We blame people. So we jump from one new circle of friends to the next, from one romantic relationship to the next. We change jobs like we change socks. We leave one church or ministry after another because of a falling-out with someone. Life becomes a revolving door with the same refrain: "What is wrong with all these people? It's their fault!"

Many years ago, after giving my life to Jesus, I learned

a valuable lesson from my friend Gregg Dedrick. I told him about someone who kept finding himself in the same situation. He jumped from ministry to ministry, from friend group to friend group, always hoping to find better people. I could have been describing myself. I think Gregg saw in me what I was describing in someone else, and so he shared some critical advice: "If you keep finding yourself in the same movie with different actors, you're the common denominator." His words cut through all my self-protection and made me pause. I was like, "Wait! How am *I* the common denominator?" I realized the drama wasn't following me, the drama was me.

One time, Jesus went to the pool of Bethesda, where the sick and paralyzed would gather, waiting to enter a pool they believed could heal them.

> One of the men lying there had been sick for thirty-eight years. When Jesus saw him and knew he had been ill for a long time, he asked him, "Would you like to get well?"
>
> "I can't, sir," the sick man said, "for I have no one to put me into the pool when the water bubbles up. Someone else always gets there ahead of me."
>
> Jesus told him, "Stand up, pick up your mat, and walk!"
>
> Instantly, the man was healed! He rolled up his sleeping mat and began walking!
>
> —John 5:5–9 NLT

This man had been sick for thirty-eight years. That is a crazy long time, y'all.

When you are sick or in a destructive place for so long, it starts to feel like part of who you are. You get comfortable in it because it's familiar. It becomes your identity. We say we want to be free from it, and on the surface, we may mean it, but deep down we're afraid because we're unable to imagine who we are without the wounds.

When Jesus asked the man, "Would you like to get well?" you'd think the first thing out of this guy's mouth would be, "Yes!" But instead, he blamed other people for his illness: "I have no one to put me in. Someone else always gets there ahead of me." It was other people's fault, not his.

I could relate to this guy. It was so easy for me to blame my earthly father for my addiction and destructive behavior. I had lived in depression, anger, and fear for so long they had become familiar friends. I believed I couldn't quit or change and convinced myself it wasn't my fault. But really, I was just used to being broken.

I believe there was a part of this sick man by the pool that didn't really want to be healed. What stands out to me is how Jesus responded. He didn't address any of the excuses. He didn't say, "How rude and terrible of all those people!" He just looked at the man and said, "Stand up, pick up your mat, and walk!" (John 5:8 NLT). I don't imagine Jesus was speaking softly to this man. I picture him saying—to that guy, and to us—"Get over yourself! I love you, but I'm not going to let you lie here in your excuses. Get up and walk!"

In that moment, this man who had been paralyzed most of his life went from broken to healed. We don't know what happened in his life after he was healed, but we do know he told others what Jesus had done for him. "The man who healed me told me, 'Pick up your mat and walk'" (John 5:11 NLT). Later, Jesus found him and told him to stop sinning. Jesus was like, "You are no longer broken, so stop breaking things."

I wonder—if broken people break things, do healed people heal things?

SHARED SCARS

One of the few good things to come from my years of brokenness was meeting Tara. Today, when I introduce her, I say, "This is my wife, Tara. She's faster, stronger, shoots rainbows out of her eyeballs, and keeps our family from falling into a dystopian nightmare."

What I'm saying is that I married up.

We started dating when she was fourteen and I was sixteen. At one point, we broke up. During our time apart, I was in the bad car wreck I mentioned previously. A drunk driver with a bunch of cocaine in his car pulled out in front me while I was going sixty miles an hour. I saw a flash of light and then

I woke up with my head stuck in the windshield of my 1990 Ford Mercury. My femur bone was broken from hitting the steering wheel. I was in such bad shape they flew me stat to the nearest hospital. Tara visited to see if I was okay. We ended up back together and have been ever since.

Want to hear something wild? Tara had corrective hip surgery when she was eight, which left her with a six-inch scar on her left hip. My accident left me with the same-size scar in exactly the same spot! Years later, when going through paperwork about my surgery, we realized my wreck happened on her birthday. If you think that's a coincidence, go ahead and hit yourself in the head with this book. There was no doubt: We were meant to be together. I believe the Lord takes what was meant for harm and uses it for our good and his glory.

Unfortunately, early on in our relationship all I did was drag Tara into my brokenness and addiction. I was the one who got her using meth. Though I would get angry and yell at her, I never hurt her physically. She tells me I would spiral into depression after becoming angry at her because I was afraid of becoming my father.

The first time our mothers met each other, they were bailing us out of jail. It goes without saying that I was not a good influence. Honestly, Tara should have left me, but she stayed, even when I weighed just 100 pounds from smoking meth and acted like a total whack job.

This might sound trite, but I'm certain I would have died

had she not stayed with me. As it was, she did stay with me, which meant she dated a dumpster fire for years.

THE VOID

If you are going through a time of pain or addiction, or if you have a loved one who is, hold on! I'm telling you my story, but remember, pain and addiction aren't where it ends.

Your story isn't over either. That may sound cheesy, but that doesn't change the fact that it's true.

Like many, I was using addiction to numb the pain of childhood wounds and trauma. Nobody sets out in life thinking, *You know what? I'm going to become a raging alcoholic and crystal-meth addict.* No. I believed a lie about who God was, so I rebelled against him, which left me broken and empty.

While it was difficult and sad, it brings such clarity to every destructive decision I made. Every destructive decision *human beings* make. We are just a bunch of broken people, making broken choices and breaking everything around us.

Choosing to live a life that runs from the goodness of God only ends with us hurting ourselves, or worse. The result is a broken person living a shattered life. But we were not made to live that way. We were meant to be not broken but whole in Christ.

The pain of living outside God's purpose is the byproduct

of a sinful, fallen world. We all have an inherent black-hole void inside that we know must be filled. But without Jesus, there's just no filling that emptiness. We try to fill it with everything but him. When we do, the hole only grows, so we get more desperate and try to shove even more stuff into it.

From the very beginning, God has been showing us: Jesus is the only light that fills the dark void.

> The earth was formless and empty, darkness was over the surface of the deep. . . . And God said, "Let there be light," and there was light.
>
> —Genesis 1:2–3

> In the beginning was the Word, and the Word was with God, and the Word was God. . . . In him was life, and the life was the light of men. The light shines in the darkness, and the darkness has not overcome it.
>
> —John 1:1, 4–5 ESV

Jesus is the only one who can satisfy the unrelenting emptiness and bring light to our darkness.

The enemy will keep whispering in your ear, *It's too late for you. You're too broken. You'll always be broken. Stay in the dark. Keep hiding in the shadows.*

Many of us have fallen for the lie that we have to stay in our mess or that it's safer there.

I just wanted to feel good and would have done anything to get there. I thought I could feel good only in the darkness. The drugs and alcohol gave me a release and euphoria that only muted my brokenness momentarily.

I mistrusted people who spoke about the good they experienced from being in the light: the joy, peace, and hope they found in Jesus. To me it was all counterfeit. My dad's violence and hypocrisy were all the evidence I needed.

I hadn't yet encountered the goodness of the living God for myself.

Perhaps you relate to my story. You may be starting to see that at the root of your rebellion and brokenness is the lie that if God is real, he's not good and doesn't want anything to do with you.

If so, I have the best news for you: Jesus can fill the void and turn the darkness to light. You may be broken, but Jesus can bring healing.

That can happen for you.

Today.

Unfortunately, I didn't turn to God to receive all that—yet. I was still too busy trying to push him away.

CHAPTER 4

DO-IT-AGAIN STORY

God saved you by his grace when you believed. And you can't take credit for this; it is a gift from God.

—EPHESIANS 2:8 NLT

My sister, Suzanne, was as wild as I was.

She is seventeen months younger than me, and in our teens she was also gorgeous and super popular, which drew lots of people to her, people I got to know who never would have hung out with me otherwise. Almost all these kids smoked cigarettes, drank alcohol, and did drugs.

As a teenager, Suzanne was arrested several times and had her fair share of near-death experiences. At eighteen, she was living with a friend in a townhouse, drinking and doing a ton of drugs. One night, she fell asleep with the television on. She abruptly woke up in the middle of the night to the sound of a TV evangelist sharing the gospel. He asked his viewers to give their lives to Jesus, and before she knew it, Suzanne was kneeling beside her bed, weeping and asking Jesus to be her Savior.

No to the Nonsense

As you know, I couldn't stomach Christians. I was the guy trying to talk people out of putting their faith in Jesus, so watching my sister accept Christ was beyond annoying. I thought, *After everything we experienced growing up with our hypocrite father, how could she fall for this nonsense? How could anyone be that gullible?*

I was so angry. I didn't want to hear about Jesus. Whenever Suzanne talked about him, she had a visible joy. In contrast, I felt like a powder keg about to explode. To my ears, the story of her newfound faith was like nails on a chalkboard, especially when she kept inviting me to church. Every time, my response was a quick, fuming "No!"

I didn't want to be around her anymore.

My friends and I relentlessly made fun of her and all her new churchy friends. It was so unbelievably irritating.

She wasn't the only one hoping I'd give my life to Jesus.

Many other people were interceding for me too, praying to God on my behalf. It's probably better that I didn't know; it would have made me even more furious. I wanted nothing to do with all that nonsense.

FIGHTING FAITH

In the summer of 2001, when I was twenty-four, Billy Graham came to Louisville, Kentucky, to lead one of his famous crusades. It was a pretty big deal. Crowds packed the biggest stadium in town for four straight nights.

My sister somehow tricked me into going. Well, it feels like I was tricked because, honestly, I cannot explain why I went. It was like an out-of-body experience. Even wilder, I used meth before going! What in the world? Just think about it: I smoked crystal meth and then drove to a Billy Graham Crusade. Who does that? I believe, despite all I was doing to run from him, the Lord was fighting for me. I'm convinced the reason I went to this event is supernatural and as much of a miracle as any I've ever experienced.

We arrived and found our seats among the sixty thousand people and turned to the stage. A band named Third Day was singing, "God of wonders beyond our galaxy, You are holy, holy."[1]

As I listened to the tens of thousands of voices singing those lyrics, something inside me was trying to break, as though God's glory were sneaking through a crack in my heart I didn't know was there. But as soon as I felt it, a more visceral emotion took over: I was filled with uncontrollable anger, a rage that made me feel like I was about to crawl out of my skin. Abruptly jumping up from my seat, I cussed and ran for the exit.

My sister ran after me, finally catching up as I was leaving the stadium. With tears in her eyes, she begged me to stay. I shouted, "&#%@ *this!* I am out of here. I just can't. I just can't be here!"

Looking back, I believe the root of my anger was demonic. The moment I heard the name of Jesus praised in that stadium, something in me snapped. It was a completely irrational and overwhelming blur of fear and fury. A lifetime of wounds and anger had just collided with the overwhelming love of Jesus, and everything within me screamed, "Run!"

Throughout Matthew's gospel, angry behavior is typical of those who are manipulated by the enemy. Here's just one example.

> When Jesus arrived on the other side of the lake, in the region of the Gadarenes, two men who were possessed by demons met him. They came out of the tombs and were so violent that no one could go through that area.
>
> They began screaming at him, "Why are you interfering with us, Son of God?"
>
> —Matthew 8:28–29 NLT

Too often, we view people who have animosity toward God as the enemy. Jesus never did. Instead of monsters, he saw two men in misery—not lost causes but sons waiting to be freed. We need to see beyond the brokenness and anger to the people Jesus loves and died for.

Just as I once did, you may be fighting against faith right now. Perhaps someone begged you to read this book and you're still wondering why you agreed. If that's you, I need you to know that you have a spiritual enemy who comes to "steal and kill and destroy" you, but Jesus came that you might have a full and overflowing life (John 10:10). The darkness hates the light (John 3:20). If you've been living in darkness, it makes sense that you would feel animosity toward Jesus. But even if you are fighting against him, he will never stop fighting for you. And I bet you have people—including the one who suggested you read this book—who are in the trenches for you.

A friend once told me they pulled over to the side of the road and bawled their eyes out for me. It wasn't about getting me to join a church, it was about getting me to God; they knew my soul was at stake.

When I travel to speak or lead worship, people often come up to me crying. They ask for prayer for their husband, wife, son, daughter, parent, or other loved one. That's amazing to me, because we are all selfish by nature. If you find yourself pulling over to the side of the road and crying over someone who is far from God, or begging people to pray for someone's salvation, pay attention to that. I'm convinced that's the Holy Spirit letting you know God wants you to continue interceding for that person. There's a reason for it; God burdens us with a purpose. I believe something special happens when we get on our knees and speak that person's name before the King of Kings. Don't stop praying!

There were so many people praying for me to come to Jesus. With all those people being led by the Holy Spirit, God was obviously up to something.

THE CASE

Remember how Saul (who later became Paul) was "breathing out murderous threats" against Christians (Acts 9:1)? It was at that point, as he was on his way to Damascus to arrest Christians, that he had a dramatic encounter when "a light from heaven flashed around him" and the risen Christ spoke to him (Acts 9:3–5). The encounter blinded Saul, and his companions had to lead him by the hand into Damascus. The Lord then spoke to a believer named Ananias and told him to go lay hands on Saul so he could see again.

How would you react if you were Ananias?

Probably the same way he did: with fear.

> "But Lord," exclaimed Ananias, "I've heard many people talk about the terrible things this man has done to the

> believers in Jerusalem! And he is authorized by the leading priests to arrest everyone who calls upon your name."
>
> —Acts 9:13–14 NLT

Ananias was afraid, thinking, *Sure, I'll lay hands on him, and then he'll kill me!*

But God insisted and Ananias obeyed. It's a good thing, because Saul became the apostle Paul, who ended up traveling all over to share the gospel and start churches—and write much of the New Testament along the way. How cool is it that Ananias got to be a part of that story?

God gave my sister, Suzanne, a burden for me to come to Jesus. I imagine that after I'd rejected all her invitations and cursed her out in public, she must have wondered whether it was worth it to keep trying. It's cool to be Ananias after you know how the story turns out, but it's easy to give up when you think you'll just suffer and maybe not see results. I am so thankful for the people who refused to give up on me.

A few months after I bolted out of that Billy Graham Crusade, Suzanne offered me a book about Jesus and I accepted it. Instead of clawing the eyes out of her head, I muttered begrudgingly, "Cool, whatever." I was still very annoyed, but somehow there was a sliver of openness starting to peek through. Underneath the anger was a very suppressed place in me crying out for help.

The book given to me was *The Case for Christ*, written by

Lee Strobel, a former *Chicago Tribune* journalist. Through the love and care of a neighbor, Lee's wife had become a believer in Jesus. Being an atheist and an investigative journalist who also had a Yale law degree, Lee decided to look for evidence to prove his wife's newfound faith wrong.

That was Lee's first mistake. In my experience, trying to prove your wife wrong usually doesn't end well. Ultimately, though, through Lee's dogged research, the evidence led him to conclude that the case for Christ was true. Jesus *is* the Son of God, who died on a cross and rose to life.

Lee gave his life to Jesus. Today, he is a nationally known speaker and bestselling author, always focusing on the gospel and the evidence that proves it true. *The Case for Christ* has been an influential book in many people's lives. But when it was handed it to me, I didn't know all that. Here is something amazing. Only recently during the writing of this book, my mom told me that I was given my father's copy of *The Case for Christ.* He had given it to my sister to give me. He knew I never would have accepted it from him.

At the time, I was living with Tara, who was then my girlfriend, in a house full of musicians. Drugs were always around. All we did was get high and play music. We had three male roommates and a few different girls who stayed over a lot. In the basement of the house, we set up a rehearsal space with microphones, drums, and amps, all surrounded by eighties-style wood-panel walls, blue shag carpet, and the stench of stale beer, dirty ashtrays, and marijuana. Sleep was an afterthought; we were too busy birthing songs and making bad choices. My roommates were all strongly anti-Christianity. We made fun of churches and people who attended them. It goes without saying, but this was not an environment conducive to accepting Jesus.

One night, I was lying in bed next to Tara when I suddenly woke up. It was 3:00 a.m. (Sidenote: What it is it about the Lord waking us up at 3:00 a.m.? Do you know what I'm talking about? It's a thing, right? I suggest we all start fasting and praying to change that time to noon. *Ha!* Anyway, where were we? Oh, yeah. I was lying in bed next to Tara.) On my other side was a nightstand with drugs all over it—and *The Case for Christ.*

I couldn't sleep, so I picked up the book and started reading about the evidence Lee Strobel discovered that established the credibility of Christ's claims and resurrection. I read about the journey to faith those facts led him on.

There are so many small things that stick out to me now as I think back on that night. Like, why did I pick up the book? It's amazing when you think about it! It just doesn't make sense without Jesus. He can raise the dead, cause the blind to see, and draw a broken young man named Stephen to read a book at three in the morning he otherwise never would have picked up.

In the middle of the night, in that dark place, Jesus revealed himself to a wounded preacher's kid.

I could not stop reading Lee's book. I was engrossed by every page. As I read, I suddenly felt an overwhelming presence. Do you know that feeling you get when you're convinced someone is in the room, even though you can't see them? It was like that, but more powerful. I cannot adequately explain what I experienced that night, but I knew beyond a shadow of a doubt that I was in the presence of the living God.

What happened next is forever etched in my mind. I began to have a conversation with God. I didn't hear an audible voice, but it felt more real than that. My mind was filled with thoughts I knew were not my own. I heard, "Stephen, I am real. I am good. I have a plan for your life."

You might be thinking those sound like the kind of words you'd pull out of a book called *Christian Things to Say*. Like, if you want to sound spiritual, just insert one of these phrases into your sentence. I get it. The words might seem a little trite because we've heard them so many times. But when God speaks a word you have heard a thousand times, even something as simple as "I love you," you are forever changed.

When God speaks and you listen, you hear him in the very core of who you are. His voice unlocks something dormant inside. It makes sense. God spoke life into existence; he said a word and planets were formed. Something that once was not, now is, simply because he said it.

When I heard the Lord say, "Stephen, I am real. I am good. I have a plan for your life," part of me felt like I had been sucker-punched in the gut with love. It went against everything I had ever believed about God.

With tears running down my face, I spoke out loud to him, "God, I want to give you my life! I want to let go of all this addiction, darkness, and anger I have lived with for so long. I want to give you my life . . . but I can't."

I could feel my heart exploding and breaking all at the same time. I was twenty-two years old and had been in addiction for more than eleven years. It felt like all I had ever known and all I would ever know. I had decided I would die at a young age because quitting drugs was not an option, and I couldn't imagine a version of my story that ended any other way. I was convinced I was trapped.

I really did want to give my life to Jesus, but it felt impossible. When I said, "But I can't," I heard God speak again. The Holy Spirit told me, "Stephen, you won't do it. I will do it." These words crashed into me like the weight of a thousand waves. The Holy Spirit told me he would do it, and I took him at his word.

Right there, that night, I put my faith in Jesus.

Before I knew it, I was on the floor sobbing and confessing Jesus as Lord. In the blink of an eye, I went from addiction to redemption, from darkness to destiny.

God did that for me.

Can you imagine being Tara and waking up to me, the guy who hated Christianity, crying uncontrollably on the floor after giving my life to Jesus? I'm pretty sure she thought I was high.

Tara was so moved after watching my life change so dramatically, she soon gave her life to Jesus as well.

QUESTIONS

God has graced me with opportunities to tell my story to thousands of people all over the world. After I share it, people sometimes have questions. I imagine you may have some questions too. I'll answer the ones I get most often.

Q: You're telling me you were saved—in a house full of drugs—with your girlfriend in bed with you?

A: Yes, that is exactly what I'm telling you.

To some churchgoing veterans, it may seem downright offensive that someone like me would have an encounter with Jesus in a place like that. It might seem like the kind of place Jesus would never show up—until you read the Bible and get to know Jesus.

Jesus was always hanging out with sinful people in sinful places. It made the religious people angry: "When the Pharisees saw this, they asked his disciples, 'Why does your teacher eat with tax collectors and sinners?' On hearing this, Jesus said, 'It is not the healthy who need a doctor, but the sick. But go and learn what this means: "I desire mercy, not sacrifice." For I have not come to call the righteous, but sinners'" (Matt. 9:11–13).

Apparently, Jesus likes to meet people right where they are, even if it's not where they should be.

Q: You say you couldn't put the book down. Why? If you were so opposed to Jesus, why did you pick it up and keep reading?

A: Great question, but I don't know. I believe it was the Holy Spirit drawing me to Jesus. Perhaps it was because of the prayers of all the people who were praying for me.

Q: So God can save even someone strung out on crystal meth?

A: Yes. God wants to save everyone and can save anyone.

At the time, I didn't have it in me to say yes to Jesus. That's why I needed the encouragement of the Holy Spirit, who said the words that changed my life: "I will do it." It was the reality of Scripture in action: "For it is by grace you have been saved, through faith—and this is not from yourselves, it is the gift of God" (Eph. 2:8).

The night I read *The Case for Christ*, it was up

to me to choose whether I would believe, and I did. When the disciples said to Jesus, "We want to perform God's works, too. What should we do?" Jesus told them, "This is the only work God wants from you: Believe in the one he has sent" (John 6:28–29 NLT).

It's also up to *you* to believe. If you've never put your faith in Jesus and what he did for you on the cross, you can do it right now. No matter what you've done or where you are. You can put this book down, just like I set down the one I was reading; you can get down on your knees, just like I fell to the floor; and you can give your life to Jesus, just like I did. This is the longing of God's heart and will change your life forever.

Q: Was it easy for you?

A: No.

When I heard the Lord say, "Stephen, I am real. I am good. I have a plan for your life," it went against everything I ever believed about God. I assumed if God had a plan for my life, it was good for him but would be a bummer for me.

Honestly, I continued to struggle with this even after putting my faith in Jesus. There have been times I've asked others for prayer and, inevitably, someone would say, "I'll pray for God's will to be done." My knee-jerk response was always, *No. Don't do that. I want the thing I'm asking you to pray about to actually happen, but God would never do that for me.* The lie that God wasn't good was *that* entrenched in my life. It took me awhile, but I finally embraced the truth that God *is* good.

There's a fascinating story about God's goodness in Exodus. When God promises Moses he will not leave the people of Israel, Moses gets bold and asks for even more: "Moses responded, 'Then show me your glorious presence.' The LORD replied, 'I will make all my goodness pass before you'" (Ex. 33:18–19 NLT).

Of all the things God could have said to describe his glory, he tells Moses, "I will make all my goodness pass before you."

God is good. It's not just a character trait, it's who he is.

I now realize that every time I sought after something good in my life, what I really wanted was God. I just didn't know it. God is good, and the very source of goodness. It's who he is, and he cannot deny who he is.

Unfortunately, I had looked for goodness in broken places where it couldn't be found. As I tried to smother all the trauma and anger of my childhood, it led me deeper into addiction. But in my bedroom that night, an overwhelming revelation of God's goodness overcame me. It was the beginning of a difficult journey to trade in the lie I believed for the truth from God.

No, it wasn't easy, and I'll share more of the struggles, and victories, in the next chapters.

Q: What about your addictions? Did you continue to struggle with those?

A: I quit everything overnight.

I told Tara we could not sleep in the same bed again until we were married. I slept on a couch for months. My friends thought I was crazy or that Tara had given me the boot for something stupid I did.

I stopped meth, marijuana, drinking, and everything else. As amazing as it is that I quit smoking meth, that feels like nothing compared with quitting cigarettes. For more than ten years, I was knocking out two packs a day. If you've been to an Alcoholics Anonymous meeting, you probably noticed no one was drinking, but almost everyone was surely smoking. Yet, somehow, I quit right away, which was a massive miracle.

To be clear, I did not feel great emotionally or

> physically right away, but that doesn't change the fact that I had a power not my own that allowed me to do what I could not do.
>
> I realize this is not everyone's story. Your desires may not miraculously disappear after you give your life to Jesus. You might need to continue fighting temptation, praying, being obedient, praying more, setting boundaries, and finding accountability. One thing is for sure: Jesus is always better than whatever temptation you're facing, and the more you chase him, the more you'll realize he has already been chasing you.
>
> I travel all over the world speaking at addiction-recovery events. After sharing my testimony, I always encourage people with the truth that, in the Gospels, Jesus never healed people the same way twice. The way he healed me may be different from the way he will heal you, but either way, Jesus heals.

Every story has a purpose. Your story is important. Hold on, even if it takes time before you experience complete freedom. And know that when you tell your story, no matter what it is, God will use it to transform someone else's.

In Hebrew, the word for "testimony" means "do-it-again

story." God wants us to share what he's done in our lives so he can create another do-it-again story.

I hope God uses my story to do that for you.

When I surrendered my whole broken mess of a life to Jesus, I had no idea my story was just getting started.

CHAPTER 5

FATHER, SON, AND BROKEN SPIRIT

For everything that is hidden will eventually be brought into the open, and every secret will be brought to light.

—MARK 4:22 NLT

You know how in some horror movies, the monster keeps coming back even after you think it's dead? Sometime in my early thirties, after I had been a Christian for many years, I heard my father's voice again, years after he'd died.

I'd found a YouTube channel where someone made videos taken from cassette tapes of sermons preached in the 1970s and 1980s at a Nazarene Bible college. Several of those sermons are by my father, Rev. G. Stuart McWhirter. When I clicked on one and listened to my father preach about living a holy life of love, it made me sick to my stomach.

A parent's role is to lead their children to the Lord by their example: "Direct your children onto the right path, and when they are older, they will not leave it" (Prov. 22:6 NLT).

Parents are also meant to be good providers and protectors. Jesus said, "You parents—if your children ask for a loaf of bread, do you give them a stone instead? Or if they ask for a fish, do you give them a snake? Of course not! So if you sinful people know how to give good gifts to your children, how much more will your heavenly Father give good gifts to those who ask him" (Matt. 7:9–11 NLT).

My father should have been that loving, protective image of God in my life, but he was the exact opposite. As I listened to his voice in those sermons, my mind flashed back to scenes from the movie of our lives.

I saw myself as a small child watching my father brutally beat my mom.

I saw her masking the bruises with makeup and long sleeves so no one would know—just one of many ways our family covered up the abuse so the monster we lived with could remain hidden.

I saw the aftermath of his tirades.

I saw all three of his children run from God and turn to drugs.

I saw myself selling drugs and smoking crystal meth, all while realizing I would die young and being fine with it.

I saw myself raging, cussing people out for believing in Jesus, and talking others out of giving their lives to him. I was leading people to hell.

As the scenes replayed in my mind, I understood why I once struggled with the idea of God as a good father. I remember thinking, *How could I ever trust a heavenly Father when I was so badly hurt by my earthly one? And can Jesus even heal those wounds?*

EVEN THAT?

I believe God heals and he still does miracles. I believe because I follow the same Jesus who "cast out the evil spirits with a simple command, and he healed all the sick" (Matt. 8:16 NLT). But what about deep wounds left by trauma? And what if those wounds are caused by a parent or a spouse, someone we should have been able to trust, someone who should have been a safe place? We all know those wounds go so much deeper.

When asked whether God can heal emotional trauma, Christians might give the knee-jerk church answer, something like, "Yes, and won't he do it!" We want to assure others—and maybe ourselves—that we're saved and believe without doubts. We tend to avoid asking difficult questions because, as Christians, we're not sure it's allowed.

My perspective is that honest faith does ask questions, but it doesn't question who God says he is. That might sound contradictory, but it's not. God wants authenticity, but at the same time we must trust him even when we're in painful experiences. When we're authentic *and* trust, God reveals the chains that bind us so we can lay them at the foot of the cross and walk away in freedom.

That's easier said than done. Especially if those chains were put there by people we once considered safe, or by a parent or spouse whom we should have been able to trust.

My father was an extremely broken man. As we traveled from church camps to revivals, I watched him preach hundreds of times and lead many to Jesus. I associated everything I knew about Jesus, the Bible, and God with my dad.

The abuse I watched him inflict on my mother seared into me the instinct to always run in the opposite direction. If he followed Jesus, I would have nothing to do with Jesus. Since my dad wasn't good, I assumed God was the same kind of father. I saw both of them through the broken lens of my pain. My fear and anger boiled in my dad's presence and at the very thought of God. My dad was all the evidence I needed that God couldn't be truly good.

Unresolved trauma became my prison. I didn't know how to be set free.

THE HIDING

Keeping the secret of Dad's abuse was our number-one rule as a family. No one could ever know.

On many occasions, my father beat my mother so badly she had bruises down her spine, arms, and neck. Although she did her best to conceal them, sometimes she ended up with a bruise that couldn't be easily hidden. I remember a time when someone at a camp meeting asked my mom about her black eye. I was young, barely tall enough to come up to her elbow, and I was overcome by dread. Would our family secret be exposed?

Before my mom could reply, my dad jumped in: "She fell in the shower."

As I heard those words, my whole body trembled with disbelief and anger. Watching my father tell a cowardly lie to protect his image, and my mom sheepishly pretend to be a dumb wife who fell in the shower, was unbearable to witness. I remember catching my sister's glance, seeing the same emotions on her face. At such a young age, I didn't know how to process any of it.

The hardest part is that even after the physical abuse stopped, my father never addressed what happened. In my childhood, his presence was massive and terrorizing, but throughout my teens and early twenties, he was there, but not really there. In the movie of our lives, he became less of a monster and more of an extra who blended into the background. His absence from my life in those years was a new and different kind of wound.

I wonder if my father's detachment was because he believed, after all he'd done, he no longer had the right to be my father. Maybe he didn't talk about the past abuse or make amends because he'd have to own what happened. He'd have to drag it out of the shadows into the light.

I imagine an abusive parent or spouse creates a new narrative in their mind, trying to erase the trauma they've caused. They construct a false reality, a self-protective bubble. Subconsciously, they might believe that if they acknowledged what they did, it would bring everything crashing down.

I don't know the answer for my dad; I only know he pretended it never happened.

But it did happen.

And at some point, for my father and for the rest of us, everything we try to hide will be laid bare. Jesus said, "For everything that is hidden will eventually be brought into the open, and every secret will be brought to light" (Mark 4:22 NLT). Everything—even the things we want to keep hidden in the dark—will be brought into the light.

That might sound scary, but it doesn't have to be. When we willingly bring those hidden things into the light to confess, repent, and make amends, they start to lose their power.

Unfortunately, my dad could never bring himself to face

what he had done. I believe this kept him imprisoned by guilt and shame.

If you relate, please know Jesus loves you and is fighting to set you free and heal every broken piece of you. This promise isn't just for sons and daughters who have been hurt. It's also for the father, mother, spouse, or anyone who has harmed others.

Jesus doesn't just heal and restore the bad things that happened to us. He also mends the unthinkable things we may have done to others. When we feel chained to guilt and shame, real healing and freedom await on the other side of a little something called repentance.

THE OTHER SIDE OF REPENTANCE

If you're thinking about what you need to repent of, it probably feels like your heart just fell into your stomach. You don't know if you should keep reading or throw this stupid book into the trash.

When most of us consider repenting, we think, *Oh, no! I can't own up. Then I'd be caught! Everyone will know what I've done. I will be canceled and become an outcast.*

If that is how we view repentance, no wonder it's become something we avoid at all costs. We shouldn't be surprised to see so many church leaders get caught in wrongdoing and exposed rather than simply confessing and repenting before anyone knew what they had done.

But what if I told you repentance equals blessing rather than shame? Does that sound too good to be true? The good news is that it's too good *not* to be true. Throughout the Bible, when repentance comes, blessing is not far behind.

In Hebrew, the word for "repentance" is *teshuvah*, which means "to return," as if turning back to something you have turned away from. Repentance is to turn from one thing to another. It is:

- To turn away from sin to the one who gives grace.
- To turn away from death to the one who is life.
- To turn away from a curse to the one who provides blessing.
- To turn away from brokenness to the one who offers healing.
- To turn away from lesser things to the one who offers everything.

Throughout the Bible, repentance is God's loving invitation to turn away from what is hurting you and turn back to him, so you can be fully alive.

It's hard to change the way we think about it, but hear this: Repentance is not about punishment, it's about restoration. God wants to rescue and revive us. Here are just a few examples:

> Those who repent will be revived by
> righteousness.
>
> —Isaiah 1:27 NLT

> If my people, who are called by my name, will humble themselves and pray and seek my face and turn from their wicked ways, then I will hear from heaven, and I will forgive their sin and will heal their land.
>
> —2 Chronicles 7:14

> Now repent of your sins and turn to God, so that your sins may be wiped away. Then times of refreshment will come from the presence of the Lord.
>
> —Acts 3:19–20 NLT

We think repentance leads to punishment, but God tells us repentance leads to blessing and revival.

It is possible that, depending on the sin, you may not get to be a pastor anymore or keep your position or platform, but you will get something way better.

Healing.

Freedom.

Restoration.

You will draw closer to the one who is the deepest longing of your soul.

Redemption is the goal; repentance is part of what gets us there. We turn back so:

- He can mend our deep, broken places.
- We can start to become who we were made to be in Jesus.
- Our heavenly Father can heal the wounds left by our earthly fathers.

Beneath my dad's horrific behavior was a gut-wrenching sadness. Despite all his horrendous flaws, I believe my father really did want Jesus but was too scared to face his demons. During the darkest years, he had pushed any real relationship with the Lord far away.

As I listened to my dad's old sermons on YouTube, I came across one he preached titled "The Unbelief of the Believer." In it, he said, "The real danger in life isn't the storms of life. The real danger in life is the danger of losing contact with the Lord."

Hearing his voice was like listening to a ghost. Though the old cassette recording crackled, the message was clear. I knew he was talking to himself, even if he didn't know it. He never did take his own advice. Instead of repenting, turning back to

God, it seemed he lost a closeness with the Lord. I believe he was saved, but never truly whole this side of eternity.

I am so thankful I went the other way, that I turned back to Jesus.

THE NEW IS HERE

In my walk with Jesus, I've learned that I don't have to beg God to be who he already says he is. If I feel like I must plead with him, "Please, God, heal me!" it may reveal I don't know him very well. Remember how I said God is looking for an honest faith that asks questions, but at the same time doesn't question who God says he is? Well, God has told us, "I am the LORD, who heals you" (Ex. 15:26).

In the Bible, one of the names for God is Jehovah Rapha, the God who heals. We can be confident in that. I have a song called "Rapha" with the lyric, "Either now or forever, we know it's gonna come. God Jehovah, Jehovah Rapha, you're our healer."[1]

That's who God is, and that's one reason he sent Jesus. Jesus came to bring healing. He said, "Come to me, all of you who are weary and carry heavy burdens, and I will give you rest" (Matt. 11:28 NLT).

A big part of healing is letting go. You are not meant to carry the weight of your past. Jesus wants to carry that for you. He invites you to release what you've held on to and cling to him instead.

In "Rapha," I sing, "We're never gonna let go of the hem of your robe," which is a reference to a woman in the New Testament who had been bleeding for twelve years. It seemed like she would be imprisoned by her sickness forever, but then she heard about Jesus and was hit by a new thought: "If I can just touch his robe, I will be healed" (Mark 5:28 NLT). Desperate to find freedom, she battled through the crowd to get close to Jesus, then quietly reached out, grabbed the hem of his robe, and was instantly healed. Jesus called her out of her hiddenness in the crowd and said, "Daughter, your faith has made you well. Go in peace. Your suffering is over" (v. 34 NLT).

That's my story.

For years, I felt like I was bleeding out from all the trauma I had gone through. But when I read Lee Strobel's book about Jesus in the middle of my addiction and anger and then experienced Jesus in a personal way, I believed, *If I can just touch his robe, I will be healed.* I battled through all the toxic beliefs I had about God, reached out for Jesus, and found freedom.

Today, I am a new creation, and my life is a testament to the fact that there is real hope for healing and redemption in Christ. There are still moments when something pops up that I must bring to Jesus and leave with him, but when I say I am a new creation, I mean it. The apostle Paul writes, "Therefore, if anyone is in Christ, the new creation has come: The old has gone, the new is here!" (2 Cor. 5:17). *The old is gone!* I believe that because I'm living proof of it.

When I go to some addiction-recovery programs, I hear people say, "I'm Bill, and I'm an alcoholic," or something along the lines of, "Be careful, because once an alcoholic, always an alcoholic." Yes, we must be wise and careful, but I'm not going to call myself an addict when God says I am a new creation. That's who I was, but not who I am. The old has gone and the new has come.

When I grasp who I really am in Christ, old wounds may try to rear their ugly heads and sin may try to tempt me, but it keeps getting easier to bring all that to the cross where it belongs.

Why? Because I am a new creation. I am a son of the living God, and my Father is the healer of all wounds.

Earlier, I raised the question, Can God heal? *Will* God heal?

My answer?

Look at my life.

I went from running from God because of my father, the traveling evangelist, to running *to* God and traveling the world as a worship leader and evangelist.

It's amazing how the Lord works. Check this out: As I listened to those words of my broken, hypocritical father—"The real danger in life isn't the storms of life. The real danger in life is the danger of losing contact with the Lord"—I felt God reminding me that it isn't the storms of my childhood that define me but the nearness of Jesus who has healed me and is still healing the deepest places within me.

Who ever would have thought God would use the words of my earthly father, recorded almost fifty years ago, to lead me closer to my heavenly Father?

God doesn't see just a few moves ahead; he sees every move, all at once, and he is Jehovah Rapha, the God who heals.

He's brought healing to my life, and he can heal you.

But there was something else I realized I had to do if I hoped to heal completely. It was the hardest part, and it's where we're going next.

Chapter 6

SEVENTY TIMES SEVEN

Peter came to him and asked, "Lord, how often should I forgive someone who sins against me? Seven times?"

"No, not seven times," Jesus replied, "but seventy times seven!"

—MATTHEW 18:21–22 NLT

In most stories there is an ultimate battle: a trial to overcome or a villain to defeat. Luke Skywalker had Darth Vader; Batman, the Joker; and Dorothy, the Wicked Witch of the West.

With my story, it may seem like my father and addiction

were the final big, bad bosses to overcome. Though the shadows they cast were prominent, neither was the real dragon I needed to slay. Mine was unforgiveness. Unforgiveness may not sound all that scary, but the pain it inflicts is unforgiving. (See what I did there?)

When you do forgive, it can reduce your stress level by up to 50 percent and improve your energy, mood, sleep, and overall physical vitality.[1] When you don't forgive, it increases your risk of depression, heart disease, diabetes, and other health issues.[2] Obviously, there is a significant negative impact to our physical health when we are unforgiving, but I think the spiritual dangers are even more lethal.

Unforgiveness can lead us away from the grace of God and toward a "bitter root" that "grows up to cause trouble and defile many" (Heb. 12:15). That's what makes it so uniquely destructive; the damage may have been caused by one person, but you will carry unforgiveness like a wrecking ball into every future relationship. You may not even be aware of it, but it's still there relentlessly poisoning your heart and mind.

Worst of all, unforgiveness messes with your relationship with God, with your ability to experience his love and forgiveness (1 John 4:20–21; Mark 11:25; Matt. 5:24).

I didn't realize it at first, but unforgiveness was the ultimate villain I had to take out before it took me out.

The same is probably true for you.

IT WAS TIME

About a week after I became a Christian, I realized that God was calling me to do something after I'd been set free from my addictions, something impossible: God wanted me to forgive my father. Leaving behind a life of addiction felt like a walk in the park compared with that. It seemed beyond impossible, like the one thing I truly could not do.

I don't like to admit this, but sometimes I struggle to relate to people in the Bible. It's not that I think I'm better than them—okay, well, maybe I do think that sometimes when I forget what I've been saved from. I read about the Pharisees and religious rulers and think, *Wow, these guys are so dumb! How could they believe they were so much better than other people?* I read about the disciples not understanding Jesus' teaching and think, *Come on! How can you guys miss the point of what he's saying!*

Even though I can't relate to some people in the Bible, when I considered forgiving my dad, I began to feel a lot of compassion for one rich young man.

> Just then a man came up to Jesus and asked, "Teacher, what good thing must I do to get eternal life?"
>
> "Why do you ask me about what is good?" Jesus replied. "There is only One who is good. If you want to enter life, keep the commandments."

"Which ones?" he inquired.

Jesus replied, "'You shall not murder, you shall not commit adultery, you shall not steal, you shall not give false testimony, honor your father and mother,' and 'love your neighbor as yourself.'"

"All these I have kept," the young man said. "What do I still lack?"

Jesus answered, "If you want to be perfect, go, sell your possessions and give to the poor, and you will have treasure in heaven. Then come, follow me."

When the young man heard this, he went away sad, because he had great wealth.

—Matthew 19:16–22

Typically, it would be easy for me to question this guy. I'd say, "Jesus is offering you a better life now and eternal life later. Why would you hold on to something so relatively unimportant as wealth and risk missing out on something so much better?"

But my perspective changed when I realized God was asking me to forgive my dad. I felt like Jesus was saying to me, "If you want to be perfect, go, forgive your father, and you will have treasure in heaven. Then come, follow me."

That's when I really understood this guy's hangup with letting go and following Jesus. He had let his wealth become his identity. He didn't know how to walk away from what had defined him for so long. I had lived with anger and unforgiveness for as long as I could remember. It was like a warm blanket I didn't know how to take off. It was all I knew. It felt like home.

It also felt like justice. What my father deserved was for me not to forgive him. To forgive would mean to let go and let God. But holding on to my anger felt like justice was in my hands, and it was hard for me to release that sense of control.

It felt like more than I could bear to do what Jesus wanted me to do: forgive my father.

Was I going to walk away sad, like the rich young man?

Was I going to believe Jesus could pull me from the depths of addiction, but not the despair of unforgiveness?

MY OWN PRISON

When I was a child and throughout my teenage years, I never could have imagined forgiving my father. I constantly dreamed of a life where my mom left him, or pressed charges and had him arrested. I truly despised him with every bone in my body. How could I ever forgive this man who terrorized my childhood and brutalized my mother?

For the longest time, I couldn't see that my anger had become a prison of my own making. Jesus had set me free from my sins, but I wasn't living in that freedom because I was chained to my unforgiveness.

Forgiveness is about a debt. If someone wrongs you, they owe you a legitimate debt. But if you are the person who has been wronged, you can tear up that debt and throw it away.

In the Hebrew calendar, one year every fifty years was to be celebrated as a Year of Jubilee in which every financial debt was canceled (Lev. 25:8–55). Imagine all your debt being forgiven in one day. You might be shouting, "Amen! I cast out the spirit of MasterCard!"

When Jesus died on the cross, he was declaring a forever jubilee over our debt of sin. If we just say yes, God forgives every evil thing we've done against him.

If God could forgive us when we were at our worst—before we had a chance to apologize or ask for forgiveness—how can we stubbornly withhold forgiveness from someone else? God is the only one who has never sinned against anyone, yet he offers forgiveness to everyone. We *have* sinned against others, so who are we to hold back forgiveness from those who sin against us? Jesus makes his thoughts on this pretty clear: "Forgive others, and you will be forgiven" (Luke 6:37 NLT).

We may feel like we are getting back at the person who hurt us by staying angry; but our bitterness isn't hurting them, it's poisoning us. The amazing thing that happens when we forgive others is that it sets *us* free.

God calls all of us to forgive everyone, just as he's forgiven us—and he was telling me to forgive my dad. I realized I had imprisoned myself by not forgiving, and I had the power to free myself by simply tearing up the debt.

Paul writes about Jesus canceling our debt: "When you were spiritually dead because of your sins . . . God made you alive with Christ, and he forgave all our sins. He canceled the debt, which listed all the rules we failed to follow. He took away that record with its rules and nailed it to the cross" (Col. 2:13–14 NCV).

Jesus wasn't the exception, he was the example.

If he nailed my sin to the cross, wiping out all my debt, then I knew I had to forgive my father. Not because he deserved or earned it but because I couldn't accept God's grace and then withhold it from others.

It all made sense, but I still didn't want to forgive my dad, and it still felt impossible.

There was one problem with my hesitancy to forgive. I knew all the Jesus stuff is real! As I've said, I truly believed it. And if it's real, that means I can and must do what Jesus has called me to do. I knew Jesus could do what I could not do on my own and that it was time—time for me to show up and let Jesus show off.

THE TALK

Maybe a week after giving my life to Christ, I finally got up the nerve to go see my dad. I made the hour drive from Louisville,

Kentucky, to my parents' house in Corydon, Indiana. As I pulled into the gravel driveway, I felt like someone was twisting my insides. I quickly got out of the car to avoid prolonging the agony, but my feet felt like concrete bricks. My mind was made up, but my body wasn't so sure.

I somehow got the courage to go inside. I entered my father's bedroom, where he spent almost all his time. I say it was my father's bedroom because my mom hadn't slept in the same bed with him for as long as I could remember.

I stood there in his doorway. He stayed seated in his recliner, barely looking up at me.

"Dad," I said, "we need to talk." I took a deep breath, then it all came out: "I forgive you. I forgive you for all the years of hurting Mom, and for all the trauma you put our family through. I know you don't want to talk about this, but I have to. I believe Jesus is leading me to truly forgive you."

It felt like an out-of-body experience. It was not a fun moment, to say the least. There was no beam of light shining on us. No bird gently landed on my shoulder as Celine Dion sang quietly in the background.

Nope.

It was unbearably awkward.

My dad had a look of shocked embarrassment on his face, as if he were about to jump out of his skin. As I recall, the only thing he muttered was the word, "Okay." Maybe he believed that discussing what he had done might actually kill him.

I did it, though. I put it in the Lord's hands and forgave my father!

Don't get me wrong, I'm not saying there haven't been days since when new thoughts bubble up or old pain hits me. But when it does, I just keep bringing it to Jesus, laying it at the foot of the cross, believing he changes everything. Because he really does.

Honestly, the experience of forgiving my earthly father, on this side of eternity, was brutally uncomfortable. But I knew I did what God asked me to do and that it was significant in the Spirit.

BUT WAIT, THERE'S MORE!

I wish forgiving my dad was all God asked me to do. I felt like all of heaven watched my awkward moment of forgiving my dad and was saying, "That was crazy!" And then, like in an infomercial, God shouted, "But wait! There's more!"

Look, forgiveness is no joke, y'all. That became more real to me as things got even wilder.

After I gave my life to Jesus and forgave my dad, Tara, my soon-to-be wife, told me she believed the Lord wanted my father to baptize us. I was furious that she would even suggest such a thing. I thought, *You've got to be kidding me!* I had already forgiven him. *Can we just move on with our lives!* But

I knew actions speak louder than words, and I wasn't acting like I had forgiven him. I reluctantly agreed.

But one of the worst fights we ever had happened on our way to get baptized. "Tara," I almost growled, "I'm not going through with it."

"I am doing it with or without you," she said.

We both realized the enemy was trying to keep us from following through with something extremely important, so we made up, prayed, and continued the drive to the small Church of the Nazarene in Louisville, Kentucky, where my dad baptized us.

My mom was overwhelmed by how God had answered prayer, especially after spending so many nights praying for me to come to him. With tears running down her face, she watched in awe of God's faithfulness. I think any parent of a prodigal understands the emotional weight of such a moment.

I had gone to my father and forgiven him *and* let him baptize me and my fiancée. Surely that was enough, right?

Right?

Wrong!

Cue God saying, "But wait! There's more!"

Right after being baptized, Tara told me she felt we were supposed to let my dad perform our wedding ceremony. At that point, I started to wonder if she was just punishing me. And God? *C'mon, can you just give this forgiveness thing a rest?*

But I agreed.

On September 22, 2002, we had an outside wedding in a beautiful park surrounded by friends and family. Honestly, I was so nervous I don't fully remember all my dad said during the ceremony, but I do recall him crying. Truth is, I was fighting back tears myself.

My mom told me my father lived riddled with unbearable guilt over what he'd done, and believed it could never be undone. And how the night after my baptism, my father wept uncontrollably and told her, "I feel like God is helping me reconnect with my children and is redeeming what I had broken."

Forgiving my dad and letting him baptize us and perform our wedding ceremony were some of the hardest moments of my life. I believe Tara knew the Lord wanted me to fully lay all my hatred for my earthly father at the feet of my heavenly Father.

After all my dad did, you may be offended by the notion of my forgiving him. I don't blame you. I was offended too. But God doesn't offer grace only to those who deserve it. That's good news because none of us deserve it. The truth is, "All have sinned and fall short of the glory of God" (Rom. 3:23). God wants to redeem everything, even the seemingly unredeemable.

The grace I offered my father in forgiving him is the same grace I relied on to save me. The grace God is calling *you* to share with the person who wounded you is the same grace he used as the only possible way to save you. God offers us an ocean of grace. Why would we fight over the water?

When we give our lives to Jesus, the redemption never stops with us. It's like a pebble dropped in the ocean, meant to ripple out to become a tsunami of redemption, drenching our relationships in grace—even the ones we thought could never be redeemed.

ENCOURAGEMENT

If you have someone you need to forgive—and most of us do—may I offer you some encouragement with these four truths:

1. *When you forgive someone, you are not saying what they did is okay.* I have never condoned what my father did to my mother, including what I said on the day I forgave him. What he did was not okay. It was evil. What happened to you might have been evil as well. The apostle Paul, in the middle of addressing our need to forgive and leave justice to God, wrote, "Do not repay anyone evil for evil" (Rom. 12:17). When you forgive, you're not saying it wasn't evil. You are choosing to let it go and trust God with it.
2. *You cannot wait until you feel like forgiving to forgive.*

Some people think forgiveness is a feeling and are waiting to offer it until they feel it. If I'd waited to forgive my dad until I felt like forgiving him, I would still be waiting. Forgiveness is not a feeling, it's a decision you make to obey God. You can do that without feeling it, and when you do, God will show up in your life in a big way to support you in your obedience. Who knows, you may even experience the feeling of forgiveness.

3. *Forgiving does not always lead to restoration of the relationship.* I'm not saying you must be friends with everyone you forgive. There is a difference between forgiveness and reconciliation. Reconciliation is about restoring trust and relationship with someone. While that might be ideal, it's not always possible. The person may still pose a threat to you. If you are in danger, please seek help and get safe. If you have gotten away from a dangerous person, you can continue to stay safely away from them and still forgive them.
4. *Forgiving is not necessarily for the other person, it's for you.* I've had people tell me they can't forgive because the person who hurt them hasn't asked to be forgiven or wouldn't even want it. No. Forgiving the other person may benefit them, but it's not for them. You need to forgive the other person for your own sake. You're the one in the prison. You're the one being poisoned by unforgiveness. The apostle Paul makes God's

> perspective on this clear when he writes, "Get rid of all bitterness, rage and anger, brawling and slander, along with every form of malice. Be kind and compassionate to one another, forgiving each other, just as in Christ God forgave you" (Eph. 4:31–32).

What does God say to do with your bitterness, rage, and anger? *Get rid of it.* If you had cancer, the doctor would tell you, "We have to do everything we can to get rid of it." It doesn't matter how you got it, you need to get it out of your life in order to be healthy. Likewise, unforgiveness is a cancer. No matter how you got it, no matter what the person did to cause it, you need to get rid of it.

SEVENTY TIMES SEVEN

My father passed away of cancer in 2012. In his last days, he repeatedly asked my mom, my siblings, and me for forgiveness. "Dad, I've already forgiven you," I reminded him.

I've come to see forgiveness as a onetime decision that we may have to recommit to over and over again. Jesus taught this very thing to Peter when Peter asked him about forgiveness:

> Peter came to him and asked, "Lord, how often should I forgive someone who sins against me? Seven times?"

SEVENTY TIMES SEVEN

"No, not seven times," Jesus replied, "but seventy times seven!"

—Matthew 18:21–22 NLT

In the Bible, seven is the number of perfection. Jesus was conveying to Peter that we forgive not just once or a few times but as often as is necessary and completely. Don't be surprised if it's an ongoing process. Keep forgiving as many times as you need to.

Those verses from Matthew are easy to agree with until we actually have to forgive someone who did something that feels unforgivable. But because God forgave the unforgiveable in us, I've realized nothing is unforgivable. The good news in this hard work? Forgiveness frees both the offender and the offended. In my dad's last days, I experienced that freedom for myself and for him.

I remember sitting in the hospital room with my mom as my dad lay dying. We knew it wouldn't be long. It's funny what you remember in those last moments: the whiteboard hanging on the wall showing the schedule of nurses assigned to the room, the familiar hospital smell—like someone had used a little too much cleaner on the linoleum floor—the monotonous low beeping from my father's heart monitor, footsteps walking by, and a hushed conversation in the hallway.

My mother got up and left the room for a couple of minutes, telling me she'd be back soon. In that time I witnessed my father take his last breaths. In those final seconds, as he tried to hold on a little longer, one of the last things he heard was me saying, "I love you and I forgive you." Then I watched his soul leave his body.

This figure who had overshadowed much of my life was present on earth one moment and an empty shell the next. In the very last moment of his life, I forgave my earthly father again. On this side of eternity, I'm sure the wounds he caused will try to resurface, and I'll have to continue forgiving him seventy times seven.

CHAPTER 7

NEVER BEEN THIS WAY BEFORE

When you see the ark of the covenant of the LORD your God, and the Levitical priests carrying it, you are to move out from your positions and follow it. Then you will know which way to go, since you have never been this way before.

—JOSHUA 3:3–4

Brace yourself: It's confession time. If you had a high opinion of me, it's about to die a thousand deaths, because . . .

I am a Trekkie.

It feels so good to drag that out into the light.

If you're like, "Wait, *what?*" because you have no idea what a Trekkie is, you're probably a cool person who has a life. A Trekkie is a fan of the sci-fi franchise Star Trek. Don't be so shocked! It only takes hanging out with me for a few seconds to realize I am a total nerd.

The intro to the original 1960s show always ended with Captain Kirk's iconic phrase, "To boldly go where no man has gone before." That is exactly what it felt like for me, in my early twenties, as I went from living in addiction and self-destruction to living for Jesus. As I entered this new world, I can't say I was ready to "boldly go." But I was ready to "scared-out-of-my-mind go" wherever Jesus would lead. I followed him as closely as I knew how because I had never gone this way before.

When I gave my life to Christ, it was like a veil had been lifted. I was unplugged from the matrix. I could finally see the truth and was ready to share it with everyone who would listen. I knew that Jesus is Lord and "salvation is found in no one else, for there is no other name under heaven given to mankind by which we must be saved" (Acts 4:12).

I remember running to all my addict friends like a crazy person, enthusiastically telling them, "It's real! It's all real! Jesus is real!"

In hindsight, I might have been a little over the top. I was probably super annoying. But what else could I be! I had gone from death to life. I now knew it was *all real!*

As you might have guessed, my circle of so-called friends

very quickly vanished. I shouldn't have been surprised. Since I was no longer the guy getting everyone high, I was now considered a buzzkill. Someone even told me, "Bro, you are being brainwashed!"

I countered, "If I'm being brainwashed, then I'm good with it, because I'm sober and legitimately happy for the first time in my life."

I felt like Peter when Jesus told him he wouldn't be spiritually clean if he didn't let Jesus wash his feet. Peter essentially said, "Wash all of me then!" (John 13:9). If giving my life to Jesus meant I was being brainwashed, then I didn't want him to wash just some of my brain, I wanted him to wash every part of it, because I was finally coming alive!

ALL OR ONE, ONE OR ALL

I know now what Jesus meant when he said, "You will be hated by all for my name's sake" (Matt. 10:22 ESV). I can't say I was fully hated, but I was no longer welcomed by the people I'd done life with for years. I thought they were my friends, so I was really hurt when they stopped talking to me. It was such an amazing time in my life, but also a sad season because so many of my friends wanted nothing to do with me, or with Jesus.

Looking back, I can see that the Lord was protecting me.

I wanted to lead them all to Jesus, but my faith was new, and if I'd kept doing life with them, they might have led me away from Jesus instead.

But I finally understood that the "life" I was living before wasn't real life at all. It was counterfeit, and I had to leave it behind. The addiction and destruction lured me in with the false promise of making me feel alive and happy, but when I came off the high, all they actually ever did was leave me worse off than before, making me feel dead inside.

When I finally experienced what being truly alive felt like, I had to share the good news with all the people I knew. What else could I do after finding out it was all real? I wanted them to experience it too.

I will always go to as many people as possible and tell them about Jesus. But I cannot be surprised if I go to a thousand and only a hundred come to him, or to a hundred for only one. Honestly, there is no such thing as "only" one, because every single person has vast kingdom importance. Each person is forever and can influence so many more people. I love how author C. S. Lewis put it: "There are no *ordinary* people. You have never talked to a mere mortal."[1] Every person you meet matters because they are all made in the image of God (Gen. 1:26).

Looking back over the twenty-four years since I gave my life to Christ, I have a greater understanding of what he meant when he said, "For the gate is wide and the way is easy that leads to destruction, and those who enter by it are many. For the gate is narrow and the way is hard that leads to life, and those who find it are few" (Matt. 7:13–14 ESV).

We cannot be shocked that a fallen world, the same world that crucified Christ, would deny him. There is overwhelming joy in the Lord, but there is also sorrow for those who turn away when he calls out to them. I was sad and disappointed that most of the people from that time in my life didn't come to Jesus, but I never let their rejection turn me away from where God was leading me. I was ready for the great unknown.

THAT'S NOT ME, RIGHT?

When I came to Jesus, I was twenty-two and delivering pizzas for a living. I was content and grateful just to be sober and saved. I also sang and played acoustic guitar in a band. We played a few shows at local dives in Louisville, Kentucky. Nothing big.

When I was out delivering pizza, all I did was listen to music, come up with song ideas for the band, and call venues to try to book gigs. Besides my pizza-delivery expertise, music was all I really knew. I was simply trying to pay the bills and live for Jesus.

One day, a friend of Tara's reached out to tell her about an ad for a worship leader they'd seen in the newspaper. That's right, I lived during a time when people still read newspapers. Tara told me that a United Methodist Church was looking to hire someone for their contemporary service. I didn't even know what "contemporary service" meant! I thought, *Am I really going to consider working in ministry, after all I witnessed throughout my childhood? I love Jesus and all, but that's not me, right?*

Can you guess what happened next? Yep, someone else called to tell me they had seen the same ad. Tara encouraged me to at least go talk to the church to see what God might be up to.

When I met with the pastor, I thought, *There is no way this guy is gonna hire me.* I figured if anything looks bad on a job resume, it's "former meth addict." I guess I shouldn't have underestimated how hard up a church can be for a worship leader because the guy hired me on the spot. It all happened so fast. It felt like someone threw a guitar on me and said, "Lead worship!" and I was like, "Wait, *what!*"

Built around the 1930s, the Silver Street UMC in New Albany, Indiana, smelled like the remnant of a thousand Sunday schools and chili potlucks. The building featured stained-glass windows, traditional wooden pews, and 1970s pea-green carpet—the type of sanctuary I often sat in as a kid to watch my dad preach. I always got in trouble for making noise. Ironically, it was usually for humming or singing while drawing on an offering envelope. If you had told that kid he would one day work in a place like that, he would have run out the door like he stole something! God has a pretty good sense of humor.

It was a very small church. The early Sunday-morning traditional service had an attendance of about eighty people. The contemporary service, which I would be leading later in the morning, welcomed about twenty congregants.

I will never forget the day I started. When I arrived for my first staff meeting, the pastor slid a piece of paper across the table to me. I looked at it and realized it was a list of songs I was allowed to play. The coolest one on the list was "I Can Only Imagine" by MercyMe.

Remember, I played in a hardcore metal band as a teenager. I played bass guitar and screamed my head off every night while people beat each other up in front of me in mosh pits. You "can only imagine" how wild it was to go from that to singing these contemporary worship songs. The amazing thing is, I was excited to play them! After the encounter I'd had with God, I was beyond grateful to sing anything for him. It wasn't that I had to sing these songs but that I got to!

That was my introduction to full-time ministry. It's funny how God works. Often the things we run the farthest from somehow end up being what we are destined for. We can't see what God sees, and we think we know best, so we go off in another direction. We can't imagine there is someone who knows what we need better than we do. I suppose that's why it takes faith to follow his lead. Hindsight has taught me that God doesn't see just a million moves ahead, he sees every move, and where he is leading is good, because "you are good, and what you do is good" (Ps. 119:68).

God is loving and kind and faithful and will not deny who he is. It's safe to say, following his lead is better than following my own.

MOVING ON

After leading worship at the United Methodist church for about four years, I was ready to move on. I wasn't aggressively looking for a new job, but still I was eager to lead worship at another church.

A friend who owned a music-equipment store told a new church startup about me. It didn't take much for me to accept a position as their worship leader. They met in a movie theater, which sounded fun and was a far cry from the old church building I'd been in. Every Sunday we had to load in, set up, and tear down. It was hard work, but I loved it.

We grew, eventually moving into a building, and kept growing. I so appreciate that time because it was a critical season for me to learn how to lead others.

Yet after about seven years on staff there, I noticed something was off. I loved the people at the church, but I felt like I was starting to slip away from what I'd felt that night I first encountered Jesus. It seemed every weekend service had become more of a production and performance I had to manage rather than a time for genuine worship.

Looking back, I suppose I just started to fall into the routine of what I thought a good church parishioner looked like. I followed all the seemingly correct "church rules." I caught myself leaning more on the teachings of a certain Christian author rather than the Bible. I would ask what such and such a worship pastor might do, rather than what Jesus might want to do through me. I had put myself in a fishbowl, swimming in circles, waiting for the next bigger church to hire me, trying to climb the contemporary-church-worship-leader ladder. I was leading my life where I thought I should go. I forgot that where Jesus wants to lead me is a place I've never been and can't get to without his leading the way.

As I felt the impending doom of burnout, I started to learn how to fast, pray, and seek the Lord in a way I hadn't before. I went for all-day walks in the woods, where I spent time simply trying to listen to the Lord. I even rented a tiny one-room cabin on a lake in Indiana with no television, internet, phone, or other people. It was just me and Jesus. I read the Gospel of John over and over again. I can't explain why, but I felt led to read that book on repeat. I journaled, walked, prayed, and simply worshiped Jesus. One day, during one of my walks, a thought hit me that I believe was from the Lord. Suddenly, I knew what he wanted me to do. It would take faith, which, as I was discovering, is spelled R-I-S-K. Faith in a big God always leads to taking big chances for him. I knew it would cost me something, but like anything Jesus calls us to, I knew the risk would be worth it.

I believed the Lord was calling me to start writing music, traveling as an itinerant worship leader, and sharing my testimony. I knew it really was from him because I was scared stupid about the whole idea. But I didn't know where to even begin. I had zero connections in the Christian songwriting community and I didn't know anyone in the music industry in Nashville, Tennessee. It felt like the most irresponsible decision ever.

Disclaimer: Not every sudden urge for an occupation shift is from the Lord. And I'm not saying only risky decisions are from Jesus, but I know safe choices are not always the right ones either. It never takes faith to play it safe.

At the time, Tara and I had two little boys, and we depended on my income. I asked Tara to pray with me about it, and after we did, we both agreed this was where the Lord was leading us.

I have one of the most supportive and loving wives you will ever meet. I can't think of too many spouses who, when their husband says, "The Lord told me to quit my job," would respond, "Awesome! Let's go!" Nevertheless, with almost no trepidation, that's exactly what she did.

I didn't go to the pastor and announce, "Stephen out!"

(Cue mic drop.) No, I went to this man, who remains a close friend today, and asked him to pray with me about it. He did and then came back with full support for what God was calling me into.

When I stepped down from my position, a friend told me something that's stuck with me ever since: "Stephen, the best fruit is the farthest out on the limb." Those words encouraged me, but I still had questions. How much weight can the limb hold? Can I know what the fruit is before I start climbing out?

I knew this new endeavor was from the Lord, but I was still freaking out inside. As I stepped out in faith, I could sympathize with Peter's fears when Jesus, who miraculously stood on storm-tossed waters, invited him to step out of the boat: "'Come.' And Peter left the boat and walked on the water to Jesus. But when Peter saw the wind and the waves, he became afraid and began to sink. He shouted, 'Lord, save me!' Immediately Jesus reached out his hand and caught Peter. Jesus said, 'Your faith is small. Why did you doubt?'" (Matt. 14:29–31 NCV).

In the months after leaving the movie-theater church, I did my fair share of getting distracted by and worried about the wind and waves. Many people warned me I was making a big mistake and setting back my "career" in ministry. I had to remind myself I didn't start following Jesus as a career move. I gave him my life because he is life. I figured if he is the way, he should lead the way too.

I'd be surprised if the other disciples who were in the boat with Peter were chanting his name and shouting, "Jump in! Go for it, man!" I'm pretty confident they were probably saying something like, "Are you crazy? You're gonna drown!"

I had to keep my eyes on Jesus as I faced uncharted waters, or I too would start to sink.

NEVER BEEN THIS WAY

I love the story in the Old Testament about the people of God preparing to cross the Jordan River into their destiny, the promised land. This was it! They had been wandering in the wilderness for forty years, and finally they were going to experience the reality of the promise God had made.

But how would they cross the water? Joshua addressed the people: "When you see the ark of the covenant of the LORD your God, and the Levitical priests carrying it, you are to move out from your positions and follow it. Then you will know which way to go, since you have never been this way before" (Josh. 3:3–4).

The ark was a gold-covered wooden chest that contained sacred items and represented the presence of God among his people. In telling the people to follow the ark, Joshua was urging them to follow the Lord, because only he could lead them into the promised land.

When we follow Jesus, we are following the one who is the way, the truth, and the life (John 14:6). On this side of eternity, we will always need to turn to him and say, "Lead me, Jesus, because I have never been this way before." If we will slow down to wait and listen, the Lord wants to speak and lead us into his good and beautiful plan.

Where he was leading me was all new, and I for sure needed him. And he was about to clearly reveal a clue to my kingdom destiny, which he had placed literally within my name.

CHAPTER 8

YOU HAVE A KINGDOM DESTINY

Before I formed you in the womb I knew you,
before you were born I set you apart.

—JEREMIAH 1:5

God has a divine purpose for your life, a kingdom calling that he whispered into your soul before time began.

It's a passion you can't seem to shake, a constant theme swirling in the background of your life. You might wish it would just go away, because it may seem silly or unattainable. But the Lord placed that longing deep in your DNA for a reason. The more you run from it, the more miserable you will become. The more you try to push it away, the more it will claw at you from the inside.

Trust me! I know all too well what I'm talking about.

AN UNSTOPPABLE FORCE

As far back as I can remember, music has always been that burning desire for me. Even when I was little, I would sing into a hairbrush, which is ironic because I'm now bald. Very funny, God.

When I was around eight years old, I set up all the couch pillows like a drum kit on the floor of our living room, and took the wooden rods out of my dad's suit hangers and used them as drumsticks. As I recall, he was not a fan of that.

I've always been drawn to music. From the time I was young, it was a seemingly unstoppable force.

One night when I was thirteen, my friends and I were getting high and listening to Metallica's *The Black Album* when one of my friends said, "Let's start a band and play these songs." Everything in me jumped up, and I responded with a resounding "Yes!" I wanted to be in a band so badly. There was just one small problem. I didn't know how to play a musical instrument. What was I going to say? "Wait till you guys hear me play the couch pillows!"

After I enthusiastically agreed, my friend gave me a perplexed look. He had been to my house and had never seen a musical instrument. He asked with a tone of confusion, "Stephen, what instrument do you play?"

Panic set in. What was I going to say? I thought if I told the truth my chances of making metal history would be lost forever! As I scrambled for an answer to my friend's question, I saw it! Behind him, duct taped to the wall, was a poster of Nikki Sixx from Mötley Crüe, playing a bass guitar. I looked closer and saw only four strings as opposed to the six I always saw on a regular guitar. In my drug-induced stupor, I thought, *Only four strings? Well, how hard can that be?*

Like watching a car wreck in slow motion, before I knew what was happening, the following lie came rolling out of my mouth: "I play bass guitar." I think I said it twice like I was letting myself know as well: "That's right, I play bass."

Suddenly, the whole thing snowballed. Before I knew it, we had scheduled our first band practice the following week. Gulp!

When I got home the next morning, I was acting nervous, like I had just murdered someone and needed help hiding the body. I begged my mom to help me buy a bass guitar. Amazingly, she agreed. I had turned her into an accomplice in my deception!

I had only two days to learn how to play. Like a training montage in some bad eighties movie, I sat down with the bass, plugged it in, and turned up the volume on my new amp. That's when the scene jumps forward to my looking like a deer in the headlights at our band practice, hitting every note but the right ones. The rest of the band just stared awkwardly at me.

My friends, who, unlike me, could actually play musical instruments, said, "You don't play bass, do you, Stephen?" After fumbling my way through only half of one song, I was kicked out of my first band.

In all fairness, I did it to myself. But that moment led me to go home and become the best bass player I could be. I practiced till my calluses had calluses. I had embarrassed myself so badly with that stupid lie about playing bass, but that moment caused me to work hard to make sure I would never have to lie about it again. (Oh, yeah, and, of course, lying is bad.)

I quickly started to teach myself as much as possible. My mom will tell you I practiced till my fingers bled. Today, I sing "Come Jesus Come" every night, but the first song I learned, by practicing day in and day out, was "Am I Evil?" by Metallica. Talk about coming a long way! With all the practice, it wasn't long until I finally legitimately joined a band.

When I was almost fifteen, I played my first show at a place called the Eagles Club, a veterans' hall in Corydon, Indiana. Typically, they hosted bingo nights. I remember maybe twenty people showing up that night. It was hands down one of the most terrifying experiences of my life! I was paralyzed with anxiety and dread. My feet never moved from their starting positions. Outside of my fingers moving, I was motionless for forty-five straight minutes. Today, I remember almost nothing from that show. I think I blocked it out because of how traumatic it was.

I eventually got past the nerves, and playing shows became my favorite thing to do. I fed off the adrenaline. We played metal and hardcore music. It was a lot of screaming, jumping, and watching people beat each other up in the mosh pit in front of the stage.

Oh, yeah. There were also lots of drugs and alcohol involved.

When I was seventeen, I went on my first "tour." We traveled from Louisville, Kentucky, to Rochester, New York, where we opened for four shows of an Ozzy Osbourne tribute band called Crazy Train. (Imagine *Saturday Night Live*'s Chris Farley dressed like Ozzy and you get the idea.) It was totally cheesy, but also a dream come true. All I wanted was to be in a famous rock band. I was convinced it was my destiny, but of course I was seeing it all through a very broken lens.

WELL DONE

In my late teens, I started teaching myself to play acoustic guitar and sing—really sing, not just scream like I'd stepped on a Lego. I even started trying to write songs. Just enough people told me I was good that their praise kept me going.

Throughout all my years of addiction, music was a constant in my life. Other than my next high, it was always on my mind.

But music and I developed a love-hate relationship. I was passionate about it and had big aspirations for where it would take me, but it never met those expectations and became a constant source of disappointment. I felt like I kept slamming into one brick wall after another.

In my early twenties, I got a "manager," a guy who claimed he managed bands but really didn't know what he was doing. I still listened to him. He told me the musicians I was playing with were holding me back and needed to go if I really wanted to "make it." So I left them and got a whole new band. I wanted so badly to be successful in music, I was willing to throw aside people I cared about. I'm not proud of that. A few years later, after coming to Jesus, I reached out to them, repenting and asking for forgiveness. Half accepted it and the others said, "!&$% off!" I suppose I had it coming.

After leaving the one band and assembling a new one, I released an album. The style was singer-songwriter meets alternative-country. It was a bit of a different direction from the metal band in which I was the backup screamer. With this new group, I was the lead singer and wrote all the songs. I put everything I had into the project. I'll never forget when a local newspaper reviewed the album. With the brutal ease of a Disney villain, the journalist wrote, "This guy needs to learn to sing." I was so crushed I saw a counselor about it. That may sound dramatic, but that's how easily wounded I was about music. I kept fighting for something that kept hurting me. I never stopped to ask myself why I had this unrelenting need to be validated as a musician.

We all like to hear "good job," but there are some areas in our lives where we pursue affirmation harder than others, and it stings worse when we don't find it. Perhaps sometimes that's a sign of a divine calling from God.

It could be that a "tortured poet" is tortured only because they are trying to understand a gift that will only ever make sense when surrendered to Jesus. I believe our destinies are given to us for a kingdom purpose. The Lord breathes into us an overwhelming longing to hear him say the words, "Well done."

When Jesus talked with his disciples about his glorious return to earth at the end of time, he did so by telling several stories called parables. In one story, the parable of the talents, he said, "For [my return] will be like a man going on a journey, who called his servants and entrusted to them his property" (Matt. 25:14 ESV). In this parable, three servants receive "talents," which was a unit of money worth about twenty years' wages for a laborer. Think of it as a big bag of gold. The servants were to steward what the master had given them while he was away: "To one he gave five talents, to another two, to another one, to each according to his ability" (v. 15 ESV).

When the master returned from his journey, he found that the first two servants had stewarded well what he had given them. But the third didn't do anything to steward his talent; instead, he buried it. The master was very upset with that servant, but the other two heard the words every soul longs to hear: "Well done, good and faithful servant" (v. 23 ESV).

Often the area in our lives where we feel the most broken by discouraging words is directly connected to our kingdom destiny: the purpose we've been given by the Lord that will glorify Jesus and bring us real fulfillment. I believe this is part of the reason we so badly want to hear that we've done a good a job when we use our "talents." But that eternal desire will never be met by this world. We will only find fulfillment and our souls will only ever be truly satisfied in hearing Jesus say, "Well done, good and faithful servant."

We can also affirm that gifting and destiny in others. We never know when someone is about to give up, so we need to take every chance we can get to speak life. The person we encourage may be fighting for their destiny.

HE LOVES YOU TOO MUCH

So many things try to derail God's purpose for our lives.

Lurking in the back of my mind was a fear of getting too old to see my dream come true. You know the lie: "If you don't get there before a certain age, it's too late." By the time I was in my midthirties, I slowly felt my chances of "making it" (whatever that means) slipping away. It felt like an impending doom. I know now that, had things gone the way I wanted when I wanted, I would have reached new levels of misery and self-destruction. Ultimately, I was viewing my love for music through a broken lens again.

One Sunday morning, Tara and I were driving to a church service, talking about how it felt like my pursuit of making it in music was coming up against brick wall after brick wall. When we got to church, the sermon was about how sometimes the Lord puts a wall up to protect us. We walked out of that service knowing God was speaking to us, so we changed how we prayed. Instead of asking him to bless our plans, we prayed to follow his. We were beginning to learn what it means to want his will over our own.

If you ever feel like you'll never get there and wonder whether God even wants you to get there in the first place, you're not alone. If you genuinely seek his will for your life, he won't let you enter your destiny until your character is ready. He loves you too much. If you arrive before you're ready, you will only hurt yourself and others. It would crush you even more than all the disappointments you went through.

Even when it doesn't make sense, trust his timing. Jesus can do more with your life in the eleventh hour than you can in an entire lifetime without him.

THE CREST

My perspective on music drastically shifted when I gave my life to Jesus. I felt true gratitude singing to him. I didn't care how campy the song was, if I was singing to Jesus, all was right in the world.

But don't get me wrong; while I might have left a life of addiction behind, I was still carrying something toxic that had to go. I couldn't seem to shake the need to be seen as a successful musician. Soon it poisoned me as a worship leader. The thrill of just worshiping the Lord began to fade into the background of my need to climb the mountain of church worship leader.

Never content with where God had me, I was always looking at bigger churches with more money and people, and finding myself seeking them over God's will for my life.

When I was the worship leader for the movie-theater church, it was small but healthy and growing. Nevertheless, I started applying to bigger churches because I wanted to be seen as successful. It's sad but true that many of us start out grateful to God for leading us to a new chapter in life, only to immediately start comparing it with something else we think is better. Back then, I would have told you I was serving the Lord, but really, I was still making music an idol.

God was about to show me the real reason I was so drawn to music.

As far back as I could remember, the McWhirter family crest hung on the living room wall of my childhood homes. My dad was always pointing it out, but I pretty much tried to tune out everything he said. To me, it was another pretentious part of my dad's false narrative. Ultimately, this crest stayed in the periphery of my life. I never looked at it because I just didn't care.

Years ago, Tara gave me a beautifully framed version of my family crest for my birthday. She hung it above the desk in my office, directly in my line of sight. I was forced to actually look at this thing for the first time. I'll never forget the day God revealed to me the kingdom importance of my family crest. I was sitting at my desk, reading the passage in 2 Kings where Jehoshaphat, the king of Judah, and the kings of Israel and Edom joined forces to fight against Moab. In their journey, they came to a place that had no water for the men or horses. The armies panicked, believing they could not continue without water. King Jehoshaphat asked,

> "Is there no prophet of the LORD here, through whom we may inquire of the LORD?"
>
> An officer of the king of Israel answered, "Elisha son of Shaphat is here. . . ."

> So the king of Israel and Jehoshaphat and the king of Edom went down to him. . . .
>
> Elisha said, ". . . But now bring me a harpist."
>
> While the harpist was playing, the hand of the LORD came on Elisha.
>
> —2 Kings 3:11–12, 14–15

As I read the words, "While the harpist was playing, the hand of the LORD came on Elisha," I lifted my head and saw a harp at the top of my family crest. I felt a wave of cold chills rush over my body. Under the harp was the Latin phrase *Te Deum laudamus*. I quickly looked up the translation, which is "We praise you, God." At that point, I was about to fall out of my seat. Then for the first time in my life, I looked up the meaning of my last name.

Turns out McWhirter is the Anglicization of the Scottish Gaelic *Mac an Chruiteir*, which translates to "son of the harpist." As I read that, I started weeping and laughing at the same time from shock and awe! God had just bombarded my heart with a revelation that felt like a seismic shift to everything I believed about the role of music in my life. He showed me that music was written into my name with a very specific purpose. Before I was ever born, I was destined to worship Jesus and lead others to him. My mind was blown! From generation to generation, my last name has carried God's kingdom purpose for my life.

AWAKENED

Your kingdom purpose is intricately woven throughout your story and may even hang from branches of your family tree. As I've said, we each have a kingdom destiny, a calling from God that is often revealed by a consistent theme throughout our lives. My consistent theme was music, but I had been viewing my desire for music from the perspective of a fallen world. Like many of us, I experienced one hurt after another because I was trying to fulfill my longing in a broken way.

If you feel the Lord speaking to you through this, then be encouraged. He wants to awaken what's asleep in you through your kingdom longing.

One of the first steps in letting the Lord reveal your kingdom destiny is to annihilate everything you think you've figured out about yourself and what you want most. Ask the Holy Spirit to show you the real thing.

It goes without saying that the cornerstone of your kingdom purpose is to love Jesus and others. But how, specifically, are you supposed to do that on this earth? It's a gifting and calling that has gravitational pull.

It could be that you've struggled to do what you feel called to and it's left you feeling jaded and bitter. You may have even let the dream die. Let the Lord remove all the layers of deception and unearth the kingdom origins of your desires. They are always from him and for him. When your kingdom calling is used for and with Jesus, walking it out fills the empty places you may not have even known existed.

My first step in unveiling my kingdom destiny took me from being the wounded son of the evangelist to the "son of the harpist," and now God was about to redeem the harpist as well.

CHAPTER 9

COME JESUS COME

We are citizens of heaven, where the Lord Jesus Christ lives. And we are eagerly waiting for him to return as our Savior.

—PHILIPPIANS 3:20 NLT

When I was a child, the Moscow Symphony Orchestra was touring the United States, so my parents took me to a performance. If you have ever heard an eighty-piece orchestra tuning their instruments simultaneously, you know it's a loud and unsettling sound, like hearing an entire orchestra falling down the stairs. All those different musicians, each doing their own thing with all those different instruments, focused only on themselves—it was a total mess. As I recall, I had my hands over my ears.

As this wall of noise continued to assault the room, a man in a tuxedo walked onto the stage. It was the conductor. All eyes were on him as he walked up to the podium. With a simple tap of his baton on the podium, silence fell, as if time itself had paused. The conductor slowly lifted his hands, and as they dropped, I heard instead of cacophony a sound so beautiful it took my breath away! I had never heard anything like it.

This serves as an important metaphor for our spiritual lives. When we, as God's children, fixate on our solo pursuits—be it personal ambitions, church activities, family matters, or business ventures—we all start sounding like that wall of chaotic noise I first heard coming from the orchestra.

But just like the orchestra after it was unified under the conductor's guidance, when we fix our eyes on the Lord—his voice, his Word, his direction, his glory, and his kingdom—we create a sound more beautiful than what I heard as a child. We start to want what he wants, love like he loves, and live for what truly matters.

Getting saved marks the beginning of our journey. Then, hopefully, there's a pivotal moment when something clicks. We are drawn even closer to Jesus and our ability to advance his kingdom is enhanced. The shift happened for me with the writing of a song called "Come Jesus Come."

THE BIRTH OF A PRAYER

You could divide my story into two big moments.

The first is when I finally got on my knees and said, "Come, Jesus, come," asking him into my life. I was born anew.

The second is when I finally understood what it means to truly long for him to return, and I prayed, "Come, Jesus, come." That prayer became a song that changed my life, but not because it went viral on social media or was on the charts for Christian radio. What mattered was how the Lord shifted my heart and taught me to long for his return with a passion I hadn't known before. The reason the song exists isn't because I was trying to write a hit but because I meant it and had to sing it. It was a prayer set to music.

Back in 2020, at the height of the COVID-19 pandemic, I was sitting at my piano with my Bible open to the last chapter of Revelation. I had simply been trying to spend time with Jesus in worship. On the final page of the Bible, I read:

> He who testifies to these things says, "Yes, I am coming soon."
>
> Amen. Come, Lord Jesus.
>
> —Revelation 22:20

In that moment, I realized I was really not good at wanting Jesus to come back. Praying for the lost to come to him, praying for the poor and widows—that made sense to me. But I had a disconnect when it came to praying for Jesus' return. When I thought of someone wanting him to return, I pictured a scary and annoyingly loud person on a street corner screaming, "Repent!" and holding up a painted sign that reads, "The end is nigh!" And that is just not me.

Obviously, I had some misconceptions about this subject.

When I dove into the theme of Christ's return in Scripture, I discovered that the cross is mentioned twenty-eight times in the New Testament. That's a lot. Thank you, Jesus, for the cross! It's how he provided atonement for our sins. It should cause us to fall on our knees in awe of God's love for us. It's so important, it's in there twenty-eight times.

But then I read that Jesus' return is referenced *318 times* in the New Testament.

Wait. What!

I'm not the world's foremost theologian, but if it's mentioned that many times, I would venture to guess it might just be more than a little important!

I don't know why Jesus' second coming is repeated so many times throughout the New Testament, but I wonder whether one reason is that the authors longed to see their friend again. Think about it: Most of them knew Jesus before the ascension. They did life together—with God, in the flesh. They missed their friend.

They also knew his return is central to God's overarching plan and longing for all creation, which can't be fulfilled until Jesus' return. The apostle Paul writes, "I press on to take hold of that for which Christ Jesus took hold of me" (Phil. 3:12). What's the goal? A few sentences later, he writes, "We are citizens of heaven, where the Lord Jesus Christ lives. And we are eagerly waiting for him to return as our Savior" (v. 20 NLT).

I get all that, but back then my thinking kept with the popular southern advice, "Don't be so heavenly minded you're no earthly good." It sounded right. The only problem was that it didn't line up with God's Word.

I had been taught not to think too much about heaven, but consider this encouragement written by the apostle Paul: "Since, then, you have been raised with Christ, set your hearts on things above, where Christ is, seated at the right hand of God. Set your minds on things above, not on earthly things. For you died, and your life is now hidden with Christ in God. When Christ, who is your life, appears, then you also will appear with him in glory" (Col. 3:1–4).

That makes me think it's not even possible to be so heavenly minded you're no earthly good. Instead, you can only be so heavenly minded you are more earthly good. I've found that:

- When you long for Jesus to return, you love people better, here and now, in anticipation of that day.
- When you pray with a genuine desire for Christ's

coming, you build things that matter more, here and now, in anticipation of that day.

- When you set your heart on Christ's appearing, you ask more important questions about how to spend your life, here and now, in anticipation of that day.

You start to ask questions like, Does what I am building matter only on this side of eternity? Am I treating people as secondary? Do I truly want them to know Jesus when he returns?

People are forever. They are what matters. Jesus died for *people*, not so I could have a record deal or get a song on the radio. And if any of that does happen, it's because he wants to use me to love people and draw them closer to him.

This brings me to the other big hangup I had about Jesus' return. You can see it when I posted a video of the song "Come Jesus Come" and, in the description, asked the question, "Do you pray for Jesus to return?" The typical negative response I got was, "No! There are too many lost people who need to be saved first!"

That's a totally normal response, especially if you have a loved one who doesn't know him. But I finally realized there's a problem with this thinking. Do I believe I love these people more than Jesus and am more concerned for them than he is? Do I think if I pray for Jesus to return, Jesus will come back and be like, "Way to go, you dummy! You prayed for me to come too soon. Now all these people are damned for eternity!"

The apostle Peter writes, "The Lord is not slow in keeping his promise, as some understand slowness. Instead he is patient with you, not wanting anyone to perish, but everyone to come to repentance" (2 Peter 3:9).

God loves the people you're concerned about far more than you ever could. You can pray for Jesus to return, knowing he won't come back until all who will accept him have. He won't lose anyone. Basically, what I'm trying to say is, I think God knows what he's doing. And we just need to pray for Jesus to come and trust God in the process.

The Journey of "Come Jesus Come"

When the Lord gave me the idea for the song "Come Jesus Come," I had just learned a lot of what I just wrote about. I was wanting to get better at longing for him to return. Besides prayer, one of the best ways I've found to reinforce something in my heart is to sing it until it sinks in. If a song I wrote ever makes you think, *I needed to hear that*, it's because I needed to hear it too. That was totally the case with "Come Jesus Come." I wasn't trying to write a hit, I just needed to sing until my heart caught up with God's. I wanted to want Jesus to return more than I already did.

I remember sitting in my basement, singing the opening lines of the song for the first time:

> Sometimes I fall
> to my knees and pray,
> "Come, Jesus, come.
> Let today be the day."

My wife, Tara, has always encouraged me with my songwriting. She plays a major role in the completion of many of my songs, mostly by sticking her head into the room and saying, "I like that!"

This time she walked in, sat down, and asked, "What is that?"

"Just an idea the Lord gave me for a song," I said. "Why? Do you like it?"

She said something along the lines of, "That is really anointed."

We started to talk about Christ's return and what it means to pray, "Come, Jesus, come." As she talked, I knew her words were lyrics:

> Sometimes I feel
> like I'm gonna break,
> but I'm holding on
> to a hope that won't fade.

Eventually, I took the idea to my friends Hank Bentley and Bryan Fowler, and the four of us crafted "Come Jesus Come." The chorus took form as we wrote with Hank and Bryan:

> Come, Jesus, come.
> We've been waiting so long
> for the day you return
> to heal every hurt
> and right every wrong.
> We need you right now.
> Come and turn this around.
> Deep down I know
> this world isn't home.
> Come, Jesus, come.

When I got the recording back from Bryan Fowler, who produced the first version, I knew it would be an important song. But an artist's favorites and the listeners' favorites are often not the same. Nathan Nockels, a music producer, once told me Matt Redman didn't really want to record "10,000 Reasons"; it just wasn't his favorite. It only went on to win a Grammy. I've come to the realization that my instincts are not always spot on. You never know which song the Lord will breathe on.

When I recorded the first version back in 2020, the label

I was with didn't show much interest. I sent it to a few radio promoters, but no one responded. I released it, but there was little to no reaction from streaming services. I became resigned to its being a song just for me and Jesus.

Fast-forward to 2022, when I randomly posted a video of the song on TikTok. It went viral, meaning a lot of people started to see and share it. When I say "a lot of people," I mean tens of thousands, which quickly became a million. The general response was not "Cool song" or "Nice voice" but an authentic desire for Jesus to return. You could feel it in people's comments: "Jesus, we need you!" "Come, Lord Jesus. Hear the cry of your people!"

I knew it was a real and holy longing for God's ultimate purpose, the final coming of Jesus as King.

The influx of followers on social media was unlike anything I had experienced. In two days, I went from having two thousand followers to several hundred thousand.

God was up to something.

Had I been in my twenties when this happened, I would have started thinking I was a big deal and bragging about how fast my platform had grown. But because God's ways are not mine, and are way better, I was in my forties before I saw that growth. The Lord had led me through enough that my character was a little more prepared for this new season. I knew the growth wasn't about me. It was obvious to me that I wasn't a big deal; the fact that I had been singing and making music for years and almost everyone could not have cared less proved that. This was not me, it was the Lord, and it was happening in his timing.

WHEN GOD'S FAVOR BECOMES A MOVEMENT

Because of God's favor on the song and the amount of attention it received, I decided to start going live on my social media platforms. I knew it needed to be pure. I never went on and said stuff like, "I'm an artist. Check out my music." Rather, I simply worshiped Jesus, shared the gospel, and gave my testimony. During these livestreams, I would ask if anyone wanted to give their lives to Jesus.

The first night, someone did. I prayed with them and sent them a message afterward to follow up.

The second night, ten people did.

On the third night, fifty people came to Christ.

From September 2022 up to this writing, more than forty thousand people have accepted Jesus. We've had Christians from all over connect with these new believers, offering next-step resources and helping them to find a local church or group of believers.

God used a song about something he wants to happen on the earth to change the earth and draw many to Jesus.

Today, the song is on Christian radio stations and is a hit by Christian-music-industry standards. The song has been recorded by Grammy-winning Christian artist CeCe Winans, and a Spanish version by Christine D'Clario, and even The Brooklyn Tabernacle Choir asked me to come sing with them for their most recent live album. Yet none of that matters compared with the fact that so many people have come to the Lord through it.

"Come Jesus Come" was nominated in the K-LOVE Fan Awards for Song of the Year in 2024. People were messaging me in droves, saying, "Love your new song!" I had to laugh, because my new song was four years old.

God's timing is clearly not mine, because it's perfect.

THE TWO LONGINGS

I believe two significant moments happen when we long for Jesus to come.

The first is the moment of salvation. It's when you believe the gospel, the good news of what Jesus did for you, that you're saved by his grace and nothing else. You can't do it, and that's okay, because he already did.

The second moment is when you join with the heart of God in crying out for Jesus' return. If "Come Jesus Come" resonates with you at all, it's because you are made to mean it.

You were created to offer your worship to Jesus, expressing in song your longing for him to return.

He came the first time so you could be fully alive, but someday he will come a second time, and "when Christ, who is your life, appears, then you also will appear with him in glory" (Col. 3:4).

Jesus is your life, and you are made to long for the day of his return, a day that will unveil the fullness of who you truly are:

- You, free from all sickness
- You, untouched by aging
- You, without a gut

Okay, that last one was for me!

While we're called to be Christ's light in this world, there's an approaching day when all that's broken will be restored: "And I heard a loud voice from the throne saying, 'Look! God's dwelling place is now among the people, and he will dwell with them. They will be his people, and God himself will be with them and be their God. "He will wipe every tear from their eyes. There will be no more death" or mourning or crying or pain, for the old order of things has passed away'" (Rev. 21:3–4).

That sounds pretty amazing, way better than whatever I have going on now. Forget about that job promotion. Forget about that new album I'm working on. Forget about your church building project.

When we pray for Jesus' return, we are praying for the speeding of the day when there is no more sorrow, pain, loss, hunger, poverty, addiction, suicide, sickness, war, or death.

Remember, when we long for that day, we love people better and build things that matter more on this side of eternity. So go ahead and put your head in the clouds where Christ is seated (Col. 3:1–3). From that place you'll begin to see what it means to truly pray, "Come, Jesus, come."

Come Jesus Come
Sometimes I fall
to my knees and pray,
"Come, Jesus, come.
Let today be the day."
Sometimes I feel
like I'm gonna break,
but I'm holding on
to a hope that won't fade.

Come, Jesus, come.
We've been waiting so long
for the day you return
to heal every hurt
and right every wrong.
We need you right now.

COME JESUS COME

Come and turn this around.
Deep down I know
this world isn't home.
Come, Jesus, come.
Come, Jesus, come.

There'll be no war
and there'll be no chains
when Jesus comes.
Let today be the day.
He'll come for the weak
and the strong just the same,
and all will believe
in the power of his name.

Come, Jesus, come.
We've been waiting so long
for the day you return
to heal every hurt
and right every wrong.
We need you right now.
Come and turn this around.
Deep down I know
this world isn't home.
Come, Jesus, come.
Come, Jesus, come.

One day he'll come,
and we'll stand face to face.
Come and lay it all down,
'cause it might be today.
The time is right now,
there's no need to wait.
Your past will be washed
by rivers of grace.

Come, Jesus, come.
We've been waiting so long
for the day you return
to heal every hurt
and right every wrong.
We need you right now.
Come and turn this around.
Deep down I know
this world isn't home.
Come, Jesus, come.
Come, Jesus, come.[1]

CHAPTER 10

THE THRESHING FLOOR

Search me, O God, and know my heart;
test me and know my anxious thoughts.
Point out anything in me that offends you,
and lead me along the path of
everlasting life.

—PSALM 139:23–24 NLT

Back before I wrote "Come Jesus Come," back when I was relentlessly pursuing success in my music career, God was trying to get me to lie down on the threshing floor. I didn't understand it at the time. It felt like I was having setback after setback. I wondered whether God was holding me back. But now I see it was a crucial step forward. I didn't know it at the time, but something important—something necessary—takes place on the threshing floor.

YOU CAN'T MOVE FORWARD UNTIL YOU LEAVE SOMETHING BEHIND

It's wild to look back over my journey as a songwriter and artist because nothing has gone the way I would have planned. Now I see this was all for the best, but that doesn't change how difficult the road has been. Many of those years felt like crushing failure, the kind of consistent crash and burn that leaves you thinking you may never get out of bed again.

Maybe you've been there too, that place where you're not sure you can take another hit. Where staying down seems safer than getting back up, only to be knocked down again.

For the longest time, I would bump into someone I hadn't seen in a while, and they'd ask me what I had been up to. I would say, "Still writing and playing music," which was almost always met with, "Oh, you're still doing that?"

I could feel the pity. When everyone else was graduating college, I was playing restaurants and bars where the customers would tell me to turn the volume down because they were trying to watch a basketball game. Talk about soul crushing.

Years ago, I was part of Iron Bell Music, a worship

collective for Iron Bell Ministries in Louisville, Kentucky. One day, a visiting songwriter and artist—someone I respected—sat me down. I was genuinely excited to spend time with this person and glean any wisdom he had to share. He looked me in the eyes and asked, "Stephen, how old are you?"

Huh?

"I'm about to turn thirty-five," I replied, unsure where this was going.

The look he gave me was probably intended as compassion but landed more like pity. "Stephen, you need to go to school and learn a trade."

Wait. What?

"Yeah, buddy, you're too old to continue with any kind of music career."

His words drove another nail into the coffin of my dreams, and they continued to echo in my head, haunting me, making every year of my life feel like a doomsday-clock countdown, always whispering that it was too late for me.

It was a lie that had to go.

Looking back, I can see how my desperate need to be seen as successful in a music career had become an idol. To be clear, I truly felt called to write songs and lead worship, so music itself wasn't the problem. The issue was that I was worshiping the gift instead of the Giver.

What I finally realized was that in those gut-wrenching seasons of heartbreak, God was asking me to let go of the idols and lies that held me back from where he wanted to lead me. He was calling me to leave something on the threshing floor.

ON THE THRESHING FLOOR

In ancient cultures, something important took place on the threshing floor, which was a circular, flat surface where grains of harvested wheat were separated from their stalks. A farmer would harness a large plank of wood, nearly door-size, to an animal such as an ox. The plank's underside had sharp, jagged rocks hammered into it. As the ox circled, dragging the weighted plank (often with someone sitting atop it for added pressure), the rocks tore and scraped the chaff (the unwanted husks) from the wheat. The farmer would then gather the wheat, leaving the chaff behind to be burned. Only the best parts of the harvest survived the threshing floor.

One of the most important prayers I've learned over the years is to ask Jesus to put *me* on the threshing floor. There, he can remove anything that might be between us, or between me and my kingdom destiny.

Yikes!

Daunting, isn't it?

In the Bible, sifting wheat is used as a metaphor for purifying and strengthening our faith through trials and suffering. Which means it's definitely not an easy thing to pray for. If the idea of praying that prayer scares you, I get it. It seems terrifying, but the outcome is always worth it. I've learned to pray this prayer because I want God to tear away all the chaff—the lies I believe, the idols I worship, and the things I mistakenly think I want or need.

After figuring out how good the threshing floor is, I wrote a song with my friends Jason Clayborn and Daniel Doss called "Threshing Floor." Here's the first verse and chorus:

> I won't run from the crushing
> I'll hold on through the pain
> What I'll lose means nothing
> Next to what I gain
> Come tear down every idol
> So this heart won't stray
> Don't let me stray
>
> I just wanna be your sanctuary
> A dwelling place for grace and mercy
> Keep sifting me till everything is
> on the threshing floor[1]

This threshing process is painful. When the lies and idols have been around long enough, I can forget who I am without them. They're like old, comfortable blankets I can't seem to part with. Yet when I let go, I realize they are filthy rags compared with what God has for me on the other side of the threshing floor. What's left is only the good stuff; it's where we finally get to experience God's beautiful plan for our lives.

FOR THE JOY

If you're struggling with the idea of inviting God to sift you, trust me, I understand how difficult it is. I'm guessing you're hesitant to tell God that you're willing to let go of what you've wanted for so long. Your desires and dreams—forever you've believed they'd fulfill you. How do you just stop thinking you need them?

You begin by accepting that what they offer is a counterfeit fulfillment. They can never deliver on what they promise. At the end of your pursuit, even if you get what you've longed for, you'll always be left wanting.

Instead, ask Jesus to shift your thoughts and desires toward what the Father wants, trusting that it's a billion times better and will fill every empty place within you. You'll never go wrong when you shift your focus from your gifts to the Giver.

You can ask Jesus for his help, knowing he understands what you're going through. The Father's plan for him included suffering and taking on all our sins on the cross, but suffering wasn't something Jesus wanted to experience. Just before his arrest, he prayed, "My Father, if it is possible, may this cup be taken from me. Yet not as I will, but as you will" (Matt. 26:39).

When we consider what Jesus endured on the cross, our trials pale in comparison. Yet despite how hard it was, Jesus trusted the Father's will. He knew that joy was waiting for him on the other side of his sacrifice: "For the joy set before him he endured the cross, scorning its shame, and sat down at the right hand of the throne of God" (Heb. 12:2).

Jesus saw beyond the suffering to his resurrection and ascension and the sending of the Holy Spirit so you and I could be his dwelling place on earth. We were made to be his sanctuary.

We have become the holy of holies, which in the Old Testament was located in the tabernacle, a travel-friendly version of what later became the temple in Jerusalem. The holy of holies was where the ark of the covenant resided and where the presence of God dwelled among his people. Now, because of Jesus' sacrifice, you and I get to be that place. That's mind blowing! We are the living, breathing dwelling place for the presence of the living God.

Verse two of "Threshing Floor" speaks to this:

> You didn't run from the calling
> Didn't push the cup away
> For the joy before you
> You endured my shame

After all that you went through
How can I ever complain
Forgive me, Lord

Jesus, forgive me for the times I thought my struggles could ever compare to what you endured for me. While we might hesitate to face our own threshing floors, we can look to Jesus' example and say to the Father, "Yet not as I will, but as you will," trusting that what awaits on the other side will be worth it.

WHAT'S ON THE THRONE?

We all have things that creep in as idols, subtly or not, to take over the thrones of our lives.

How do you know if this has happened?

Well, let's say you tell everyone you love Jesus. There's nothing in this life you care about more than him. He's all you need. But then the job you've been praying for slips through your fingers. Or that relationship you've been dreaming about doesn't materialize. Or people don't love your art. Or you don't have enough money.

Are you still good? Will you still say Jesus is enough? Or do you crumble when things go sideways or seem to fall apart? Does your "I love Jesus!" morph into "How could you let this happen to me, God!" If so, that's how you know something has crept onto the throne of your heart and become an idol.

I get it because I've been there. I have cursed at the Lord for letting *my* dreams for my life go down in flames. It took me way too long to learn that *his* dream for my life is way better than mine, and that *Jesus* is the greatest longing of my heart. He is the only thing that will ever be truly enough. Everything else leaves me empty.

LET IT FALL

I've mentioned this before, but it bears repeating: You and I are saved by grace. This isn't just a onetime event, it's an ongoing process that transforms how we live.

When you embrace the gospel, truly grasping what Jesus has done for you, you can't turn around and say, "Thanks, I'll take it from here." It doesn't work that way. When you accept his gift of salvation, it's Jesus who's saying, "I'll take it from here."

From that moment on, you're no longer living by your own righteousness. When God looks at you, he sees you covered in Jesus' righteousness. You're not called to strive for something he's already accomplished on the cross. As Jesus said when he was dying for you, "It is finished" (John 19:30).

So why does the threshing floor still matter? Because

while your salvation is secure, there may be things in your life that need to be thrown onto that floor. These things won't affect your salvation, but they can wreak havoc on your life, hurt those around you, and—perhaps most painful—grieve Jesus' heart.

This realization was the spark that ignited the lyrics for the bridge of "Threshing Floor":

> Let it fall, let it fall on the threshing floor
> Everything that's between you and me, Lord

In 2020, I started to release my own music as a solo artist. By some miracle, I scraped together enough money to hire a Nashville music producer for a six-song release titled *Grave Clothes*. I had high hopes for the title track, believing it might do well on the radio. I went all in, hiring a radio promoter and investing in marketing.

Then *Grave Clothes* dropped right as the world screeched to a halt, plunging into the throes of the COVID-19 pandemic. It came out the same week everything shut down and the globe retreated into quarantine and isolation. As you might have guessed, radio stations were not exactly clamoring to pick up new music during a mass quarantine, especially a song titled "Grave Clothes." Few to none added the song.

In the eyes of the industry, my song fell flat. I realize its subpar performance was a small thing compared with a global crisis. Still, it's gut-wrenching to pour your money, heart, and creativity into something only to see it flop.

This was not my first rodeo with disappointment. At this point, I'd released many songs that hadn't done well. And I'm ashamed to admit each setback produced an emotional breakdown, clear evidence that music still held idol status in my life.

But something was different with *Grave Clothes*. I felt secure, unshaken. I just kept worshiping Jesus and writing songs. Interestingly, it was around this time that "Come Jesus Come" (the song that would finally give me music success) began to take shape.

What changed? Before *Grave Clothes* released, I'd finally recognized I was on the threshing floor, and I could choose to cling to the chaff or let it go. Finally, I chose the latter. The process hurt, but it was worth it.

I had to go into the wilderness for a while, where I simply sang for and to Jesus. As I allowed him to tear down the idol of success in music, something beautiful happened: I began to truly enjoy creating with him. Instead of feeling a constant pressure to achieve, I simply enjoyed making music with and for Jesus.

This transformation didn't happen overnight. I had to let him take me through the process, allowing everything that stood between us to fall onto that threshing floor.

THE ONE THING

At forty-seven I am way past the typical expiration date for the music industry. Yet God has me walking through doors I never imagined possible. I have seen tens of thousands come to Christ through my story, I have a major record-label contract, my songs are on the radio, and I go on tours where I get to lead thousands of people in worshiping Jesus. And I also have a book deal—for the book you're reading right now.

I'm not bragging, because it's clearly not me; I was doing music for years with almost zero progress. Any shred of success has come by the grace of Jesus with the purpose of loving people and leading them to him. It's not my own doing, I'm simply following where he leads. There is a lightness to it all that I know is the Holy Spirit.

And perhaps most important, my identity is no longer wrapped up in any of it. First and foremost, I am a child of the living God. Second, I am a husband and father. Making music, while a blessing, comes last in the importance of my roles.

As I look back over my life so far, all I can say is I am thankful God's ways are not mine. They are way better. As good as all the things God is doing through my life might sound, none of it comes close to knowing Jesus. He's the one thing I've always wanted, even when I didn't realize it.

When you are standing in eternity, you won't be scrolling though your highlight reel of earthly accomplishments.

There will be no time to brag. You'll be too busy worshiping Jesus. In that moment, everything that ever stood between you and him will be left behind on the threshing floor. All the chaff will have fallen away, leaving only what truly matters: you with Jesus.

CHAPTER 11

WHAT WAS, WHAT IS, AND WHAT IS TO COME

"I am the Alpha and the Omega," says the Lord God, "who is, and who was, and who is to come, the Almighty."

—REVELATION 1:8

Imagine you're sitting in a packed movie theater, waiting for the film to start. You sink into the reclining chair. That first fistful of hot popcorn melts in your mouth. Suddenly, a picture of *you* pops up on the giant screen. To your dismay, it's not the flattering Photoshop version but your worst driver's license photo. (You know what I'm talking about: the one that looks like a mug shot.)

As if that weren't bad enough, after the photo, a list of

every gross and deplorable thing you've ever done slowly scrolls across the screen, like credits at the end of a movie.

What would you do? Would you scream? Puke? Run?

Now imagine this. What if you saw your picture, but then instead of the damning list of your sins, a single word fills the screen: Jesus.

If you've accepted Christ, that scenario isn't imaginary, it's reality. When God looks at you, he sees Jesus. He sees you not through the lens of your past but through the lens of Jesus' blood. This is the gospel, the good news, and we need to be reminded of it often.

Forgetting What Is Behind

I'm not sure what emotions you've felt as you've read about my life. You may have felt overwhelmed, or grateful you avoided so much of what I went through and put myself through. But it's also possible you've been trapped by your past, and the enemy can use that to hijack your present and keep you from stepping into your kingdom destiny.

The apostle Paul, a man with a dark history, writes, "One thing I do, forgetting those things which are behind and reaching forward to those things which are ahead, I press toward the goal for the prize of the upward call of God in Christ Jesus" (Phil. 3:13–14 NKJV).

This is the guy who stood in approval as a mob murdered a man named Stephen because he followed Jesus. A man named *Stephen*. Yikes!

> They rushed at him [Stephen] and dragged him out of the city and began to stone him. . . . Saul was one of the witnesses, and he agreed completely with the killing of Stephen.
>
> —Acts 7:57–58; 8:1 NLT

Saul (who later became Paul) also oversaw the persecution of many Christians: "Saul was going everywhere to destroy the church. He went from house to house, dragging out both men and women to throw them into prison" (Acts 8:3 NLT).

Can you imagine the weight of his past? When Paul talks about forgetting the things of his past and pressing on toward the goal ahead, you can trust he is sincere. If anyone knows the need to move on, it's Paul. He gets how hard it can be to let go.

I think he'd also tell us that it's really difficult to do this on our own instead of bringing it to Jesus.

In a counseling session several years ago, I finally told the story of when, as a child, I watched my father drag my mom across the floor by a belt he had wrapped around her neck. That traumatic memory had lived rent free in the back of my mind since the day it happened. It haunted me, whispering lies about my unescapable brokenness.

In that moment with my counselor, I faced a choice: Fall

deeper into the trauma of that memory, or lay it at the feet of Jesus and walk away.

I chose freedom. And you can too.

The same goes for all the horrible things I did before I knew Jesus. The promise of Scripture is this: "He has removed our sins as far from us as the east is from the west" (Ps. 103:12 NLT).

That's the good news of the gospel. You are not defined by what was. You are new. "Anyone who belongs to Christ has become a new person. The old life is gone; a new life has begun!" (2 Cor. 5:17 NLT).

The journey to healing isn't about erasing your past, it's about reclaiming your future. What happened to you is part of your story, but it doesn't have to be your destiny. In Christ, your wounds become wisdom, your scars strength, and your darkest chapters the backdrop against which God's redemptive light shines most brilliantly. Today, you can choose to step out of the shadow of what was and into the promise of what could be.

LIVING IN THE "RIGHT NOW"

Do you ever feel like you're the rope in a tug-of-war, with regret from the past pulling at you from one end and anxiety about the future from the other?

One time a pastor friend said, "You are made to live in the present with the Lord and others. Regret wants to keep us in the past, and anxiety sometimes wants to drag us into what might happen in the future. However, the Spirit of God is with you right now. He is the source of peace right now. He is the spring of living water right now."

My friend then pointed to a Bible verse: "'I am the Alpha and the Omega,' says the Lord God, 'who is, and who was, and who is to come, the Almighty'" (Rev. 1:8).

God has the whole timeline covered. You get to rest and let it fall into his hands, where it all belongs. You can live in this moment, and this moment is when you can trust him. Now is when you get to worship and be with him. One of the most important things you can give the Lord is your right now.

When God sends Moses to the people of Israel to lead them out of slavery, Moses asks the Lord what he should say when they ask who sent him.

"God replied to Moses, 'I AM WHO I AM. Say this to the people of Israel: I AM has sent me to you'" (Ex. 3:14 NLT).

God calls himself "I AM." His very name is present tense. He wants you to be with him in your right now and to let him take care of your past and future.

REACHING TOWARD WHAT'S AHEAD

If you go out and survey Christian coffee mugs and "Scripture art" on the walls of people's homes, one verse you're sure to find is "'For I know the plans I have for you,' declares the LORD, 'plans to prosper you and not to harm you, plans to give you hope and a future'" (Jer. 29:11).

Many of us read these words and think, *Wow, God is going to do something great with my life*, but we wonder what it could be. He tells us in the next verses: "Then you will call on me and come and pray to me, and I will listen to you. You will seek me and find me when you seek me with all your heart" (vv. 12–13).

The beautiful future God promises is one where you are *with him.*

The people of Israel were in exile, no longer living in the promised land, where they believed God lived in the temple. Jeremiah was telling them that their future, if they sought God, was with him.

We can apply this today in at least two ways.

First, those who accept Jesus have the Holy Spirit in them. We get to be with the Lord, talk to him, and know he hears us. We can take that for granted, but it is mind-blowingly awesome!

Second, we look forward to the final return of Jesus.

> Then I saw "a new heaven and a new earth," for the first heaven and the first earth had passed away, and there was no longer any sea. I saw the Holy City, the new Jerusalem, coming down out of heaven from God, prepared as a bride

> beautifully dressed for her husband. And I heard a loud voice from the throne saying, "Look! God's dwelling place is now among the people, and he will dwell with them. They will be his people, and God himself will be with them and be their God."
>
> —Revelation 21:1–3

A time is coming when Jesus will return, the world as we know it will end, and we will fully be with God as he is with us. For now, there is a kingdom-advancing destiny the Lord has for you. If he didn't have one, I imagine he'd just take you to be with him now. You are here for a reason. Your life matters because you have the Spirit of Jesus in you and are called to shine his light in a world that seems to have a love affair with darkness (Matt. 5:14–16).

You have a purpose, and to walk in it, you need him to lead you. "Your word is a lamp to guide my feet and a light for my path" (Ps. 119:105 NLT).

Imagine walking a dark path with only a candle or flashlight. You wouldn't be able to see the entire path because you'd have enough light only for the next step or two. That's how God leads us so we'll learn to trust him and won't run ahead of his leading. Ours is a step-by-step faith.

We live out our calling here and now while we long for then and there. That's what Paul means when he says he is "reaching forward to those things which are ahead" (Phil. 3:13

NKJV). In the next verses, he explains that what he is looking forward to is the return of Christ.

> I press on to reach the end of the race and receive the heavenly prize for which God, through Christ Jesus, is calling us. . . . We are citizens of heaven, where the Lord Jesus Christ lives. And we are eagerly waiting for him to return as our Savior. He will take our weak mortal bodies and change them into glorious bodies like his own, using the same power with which he will bring everything under his control.
>
> —Philippians 3:14, 20–21 NLT

Part of letting go and letting God redeem our past is being present with him now as we press on toward the goal of his return.

As he restores you and redeems your story, the Lord will show you what truly matters. You will see the big picture and live from real hope, joy, and peace. You'll start to love people better here and now as you wait for then and there.

When I gave my life to Jesus, I couldn't have imagined how he would redeem my story. I would have been content with a future of sobriety and a steady job. Instead, God took my life marked by shame and instead marked it with his glory.

Today, I am free. Fully alive in Christ.

That's not just a nice idea, it's the transformative power of the gospel.

- What if you could truly let go of your past?
- What if you could fully embrace God's presence right now?
- What if you could dream with God about your future?

You can. It's possible. It's available to you right now.

As you look over your entire story—what was, what is, and what will be—may you say, "Come, Jesus, come."

Your redemption story is just beginning.

ACKNOWLEDGMENTS

There are so many people I want to thank, and I'm certain to leave someone out, so I will keep it simple.

Hopefully, after you've read this book, it goes without saying, but THANK YOU, JESUS!

To my wife and three boys, Tara, Andrew, Alex, and Austin: You are the proof of God's redemption of my story. I love you guys.

Thank you to my best friend, Joel Gerdis, for cheering me on and walking with me through the process of unpacking my story.

To my brother, Stuart, and my sister, Suzanne: I love you both and know God will use what was meant for harm for good.

Mom, thank you for letting me tell this story and for being the image of grace and strength. I know God will bring only good from sharing all he has redeemed.

I'm grateful to Vince Antonucci for diving into my story and partnering with me to get this book right.

Thank you to Lee Strobel for writing the foreword to this

book and for your book *The Case for Christ,* which God used as a catalyst to redeem my life.

Thank you to Mark Mittelberg for encouraging me to publish this book and for introducing me to Don Gates, the best literary agent and champion for the stories God wants to tell.

I'm grateful for Keren Baltzer and the Zondervan team for helping me share my story.

APPENDIX 1

THE GOSPEL IS GOOD NEWS

Congratulations, you've read the whole book! Or you're one of those psychopaths who jumps to the end of the book. If this is the only chapter you read, it's a pretty good one. I believe you were given this book or drawn to it for a reason. Nothing just happens by accident. God is always fighting for your destiny, even in the details. He wants you to find out who you are fully alive in Jesus.

That's why it's a good time to clearly share the gospel, the best I know how. It's going to be simple, so don't worry. Just grab a Bible, because hopefully you won't have to buy a bunch of other books to understand it. Ultimately, the word *gospel* means "good story" or "good news." And that's exactly what it is. If you are not hearing good news, you're not hearing the gospel. So here we go.

HOW WE GOT HERE

In the garden of Eden, God made man and woman in his image (Gen. 1:27). They lived in perfect relationship with God and his creation. Everything was as he designed. There was no death, only life. All was good (v. 31).

There were two trees in the garden. One was called the tree of the knowledge of good and evil, the other the tree of life (2:9). God warned Adam and Eve, "You are free to eat from any tree in the garden; but you must not eat from the tree of the knowledge of good and evil, for when you eat from it you will certainly die" (vv. 16–17).

Then Satan came along and deceived Eve, leading her and Adam to eat from the tree of the knowledge of good and evil. Taking that bite was like telling God, "You're holding out on us." In that instant, sin entered the world.

Have you ever made a choice you thought was a good one, only to realize afterward what a terrible mistake you'd made? That moment when you'd give anything for a do-over? Adam and Eve had it as good as it gets. Then in the blink of an eye, they knew exactly what they'd lost.

After eating from the tree of the knowledge of good and evil, it was clear to them: Their righteousness would never be enough. Righteousness is all about being in right standing with God. It's like asking God, "Are we good?" Because of sin, without Jesus, the answer is clear: "Nope. We ain't good."

That's when guilt and shame kicked in (3:8–9). Again, guilt says, "I've *done* something wrong." Shame says, "I *am* something wrong." Apart from Christ, we're imprisoned in those dark places. We're depressed, angry, fearful—the list goes on. We are simply broken without him.

To eat from the tree of the knowledge of good and evil is to decide what's right or wrong apart from God. This is how we end up with mantras like "That's *my* truth." Listen, y'all, I've followed my truth, and it was a lie that only hurt me! I want the one who *is* truth. Jesus says, "I am the way and the truth and the life. No one comes to the Father except through me" (John 14:6).

He is truth. Without him, we're lost trying to figure it out on our own. We keep trying and keep missing it. We can't see that there are only two choices: life or death. In Deuteronomy 30, the Lord tells the people of Israel, "Now listen! Today I am giving you a choice between life and death" (v. 15 NLT).

It's amazing how clear that is. Yet just like Adam and Eve, we often keep choosing the latter.

I'VE GOT SOME BAD NEWS

You know how people say, "I've got good news and bad news"? Well, before I tell you the good news, I must give you the bad: Apart from Jesus, there is only death. We have God's law, which shows us how far we miss the mark without Jesus. If we kept the law perfectly, we'd be saved, but we can't. Paul writes, "For no one can ever be made right with God by doing what the law commands" (Rom. 3:20 NLT).

So the bad news: You cannot save yourself because you are incapable of doing all the right things. Your right standing (righteousness) with God is severed. You are destined for death. *Ouch!* I warned you it was bad news!

Early on in our marriage, Tara and I were your typical young couple who could barely pay the bills. Time after time, we forked over what little we had to cover the electric bill, only to come up short. We knew it wasn't enough because we would suddenly be sitting in the dark!

We all have a massive sin debt we can never pay, regardless of how good we think we are. "For all have sinned and fall short of the glory of God" (Rom. 3:23).

We can try our best to pay off the debt we owe God. Yet apart from Christ, we'll always come up short, left in the dark. There is nothing we can do.

I said I'd give you the bad news first. Now here comes the good part.

AND SOME GOOD NEWS

There's a meme that says, "'I'm sorry' and 'My bad' mean the same thing unless you're at a funeral." One says, "I am sorry for the death of your loved one." The other says, "I am to blame for the death of your loved one."

Context matters. When Jesus says, "No one comes to the Father except through me" (John 14:6), we react from our limited perspective: "It's unfair there's only one way! I should be able to choose!" But in context—remembering that we already made our choice by sinning, by eating from the tree that brings death—we realize that having only one way isn't unfair; we don't deserve a way at all. We think we're saying "I'm sorry" at a funeral, when from God's perspective we are saying "My bad." We're not just observers of the tragedy that happened to Jesus, we are responsible for it. We are guilty. Very guilty. Thank you, Father, for Jesus!

Bottom line: You need to be saved from eternal separation from the one who is life. The only way is Jesus. Don't worry! I'll explain the one thing you need to do. You read that right, there is *one* thing. But first, let me tell you just how good the good news really is.

You are separated from God for all eternity because of sin, destined for death. In the beginning, God saw all that he had made and was like, "That's good" (Gen. 1:31). When he saw you trapped in sin, he was like, "That's not good." Instead of leaving you that way, he did something about it. "For God so loved the world that he gave his one and only Son, that whoever believes in him shall not perish but have eternal life" (John 3:16).

He sent Jesus to make the sacrifice you could never make. Jesus is fully God, but also fully human. He lived a sinless life and died on the cross. His perfect blood paid that massive sin debt you could never pay. He rose from the grave, destroying the power of sin and death. He is now King and High Priest forever (Rev. 19:16; Heb. 7:24–26), and intercedes with God on your behalf (Heb. 7:25). If you have given your life to Jesus, when God looks at you, he doesn't see your mess, he sees a redeemed son or daughter (Gal. 4:5–6). He sees Jesus' righteousness (1 Cor. 1:30). That is some really good news, y'all!

And this really good news gets even better.

As if being saved by what Jesus did weren't incredible enough, he's also got this wildly good purpose for your life. Like I've said before, the gospel's target is your being fully alive. Jesus put it this way: "I have come that they may have life, and have it to the full" (John 10:10).

Let's be honest, when we hear "eternal life" we might imagine floating around on clouds playing harps for all eternity. That doesn't sound like life at all. It sounds like being bored to death! But true, everlasting life starts when you know Jesus, the one who is life. Listen to what Jesus prayed on behalf of all who believe: "Now this is eternal life: that they know you, the only true God, and Jesus Christ, whom you have sent" (John 17:3).

Like I've said, the real you is the you who is fully alive in

Jesus. That is the goal of the gospel. The you who is fully alive, here and now, is Jesus living through you. That advances the kingdom of God on earth and fulfills the deepest longings of your soul. You know those places in you that have always felt off, like something was missing? It's because something was. Jesus—the way, the truth, the life—was missing. Everything changes because of him. You go from a barren wasteland to a lush valley with rivers of living water rushing through it. This is the good news of the gospel.

WHAT MUST I DO?

After you've heard the bad news and the very good news, the question becomes, What must you do to be saved? How do you give your life to Jesus?

The answer to that question is what makes the good news so good. Like I said, the law demanded you live by an impossible list of rules. When a crowd asked Jesus what work God wanted from them, Jesus said, "The work of God is this: to believe in the one he has sent" (John 6:29).

Wait! That's it? Just believe? Jesus then clarifies, "For my Father's will is that everyone who looks to the Son and believes in him shall have eternal life, and I will raise them up at the last day" (v. 40).

Is it really that simple? The answer is yes! I know it's

true, because that's what I did more than twenty years ago. I believed Jesus. I took him at his word.

This is offensive to so many people. Something in us can't seem to handle it being that easy. Well, it wasn't. What Jesus went through on our behalf was brutal.

> And being in agony he prayed more earnestly; and his sweat became like great drops of blood falling down to the ground.
>
> —Luke 22:44 ESV

> And being found in human form, he humbled himself by becoming obedient to the point of death, even death on a cross.
>
> —Philippians 2:8 ESV

He went through what you and I deserved. He suffered so we could believe and be saved. He did what we couldn't do. The night I gave my life to Jesus, I told him I couldn't do it. He knew I meant it. So the Holy Spirit spoke into me these words: "You won't do it. I will." Just as the apostle Paul writes, "God saved you by his grace when you believed. And you can't take credit for this; it is a gift from God" (Eph. 2:8 NLT).

God did it, not me. Don't believe the lie that you now must maintain your salvation on your own, as if you make one mistake and you're out. The only thing God expects from you is to believe (John 6:29).

Let me clarify something: When you truly believe and know something is true, you act on it. If someone tells me to jump off a cliff, I'm gonna have to take a hard pass, because I believe I'll end up a human pancake. In the same way, if I believe Jesus is Lord, that belief should be evident in my life.

Yes, you are now a redeemed son or daughter, but that isn't a license to do whatever you want. Actions and words still have consequences. If I punch someone in the face, I'm headed to jail. Sure, I will be a redeemed son of God in jail, but I'm still going to reap what I sow in this life. Yet—here's the amazing part—I am still a child of God, still covered by his righteousness. Otherwise, I'm back to living under the law.

If you and I are saved by grace, the question shouldn't be, What can we get away with without crossing the line? Look at what Peter writes: "Do not conform to the evil desires you had when you lived in ignorance. But just as he who called you is holy, so be holy in all you do; for it is written: 'Be holy, because I am holy'" (1 Peter 1:14–16).

You are no longer living in ignorance. You've heard the truth and hopefully believed. Now you get to become increasingly like the one who called you. What he calls you to is not a list of things you don't get to do but a description of who you get to be. You get to be free from addiction. You get to be joyful. You get to be a son or daughter. You get to be fully alive. You get to be holy as Jesus is holy.

If you ask me, that's some really good news!

Do You Believe?

After hearing the good news, do you believe? Do you want to give your life to Jesus? If the answer is yes, pray the following prayer. Know that you are not just repeating words like a robot, you are talking to Jesus, and he longs to hear you say these words:

> *Jesus, I believe you are the Christ, the Son of the living God. You are my Lord and Savior. You died on the cross, paying the price I could never pay. You rose from the grave, making a way where there was no way. I repent of all my sins and give you my life. Fill me with your Holy Spirit. I ask these things in your powerful name, Jesus.*

If you just gave your life to him, I am proud of you and cheering you on!

I know how it feels to take those first steps. Please read the following appendix, "Now What?" for some help with next steps, because I don't want you to just say some words and disappear into the void. You matter, and the best is yet to come!

APPENDIX 2

NOW WHAT?

I pray this book has drawn you closer to Jesus. If these pages have led you to embrace the gospel, you might be wondering about your next steps. Remember, though, if you've been saved by grace, you don't need to "take it from here." There's never a part of the equation where you make yourself good enough. I know I sound like a broken record, but it's super important.

You are not called to earn or maintain your salvation. You are, however, called to mature in Christ.

BE BAPTIZED

Before we get into some of the basic things that help you grow spiritually, let me encourage you to be baptized. I'm not saying you aren't saved if there's no way for you to be baptized before you leave this earth—just look at the criminal on the cross next to Jesus' cross, who put his faith in Jesus and found salvation in his final moments (Luke 23:41–43).

Let me try to make this simple: Baptism is a declaration. As you go under the water, you are burying your old self with Christ. As you come up, you are raised to new life with him (Rom. 6:1–7). Look, there may be some arguments about this, but if Jesus was baptized (Matt. 3:13–16), then I'm getting baptized! If you can, and Jesus did, why wouldn't you? Cool!

That's enough about that. I'm sure there's a ton of books on the subject. Have at 'em! Let's get on with some next steps to help you mature in Christ.

GROW UP!

Ever wonder why you're still here after giving your life to Jesus? Why not just head straight to heaven? There is a reason: God has a destiny for your life and it's important. There never has been and never will be another "you" fully alive in Jesus. So yes, you are saved, but you must grow and mature spiritually so you can steward God's call for your life.

The author of Hebrews challenged some believers who were stalled in their spiritual growth, not moving forward in their faith.

APPENDIX 2

> You have been believers so long now that you ought to be teaching others. Instead, you need someone to teach you again the basic things about God's word. You are like babies who need milk and cannot eat solid food. For someone who lives on milk is still an infant and doesn't know how to do what is right. Solid food is for those who are mature, who through training have the skill to recognize the difference between right and wrong.
>
> —Hebrews 5:12–14 NLT

So many in today's church are content to be "fed" by a pastor or popular Bible teacher rather than spend time in the Word themselves. We are content to let someone else go up the mountain to meet with God while we wait below. But when our faith in Jesus is built on the foundation of someone else's faith, if that person falls, our foundation crumbles. On the other hand, if our faith is built on knowing Jesus personally, no matter what comes, we're on solid ground.

Don't get me wrong. You can learn from others who are farther along in their faith, just don't let your relationship with Jesus be only through them. Your faith needs deeper roots than that.

If you have given your life to Jesus, you're not meant to watch from the sidelines. The Lord is not just inviting you into the holy of holies, he has made *you* into that place. Don't miss out on spending time with him and getting to know him better. This is about developing a real, living relationship with the God who chose to make his home in you.

MATURE IN THE WORD

The Bible isn't just another book, it's God's gift to help you truly know him. The more time you spend in it, the more you're giving the Holy Spirit a library of truth to pull from. It's like building a spiritual arsenal.

When Jesus was in the wilderness, Satan (as he always does) attacked with lies and twisted versions of what God had said (Matt. 4:3–9). In response, Jesus simply quoted from the Old Testament book of Deuteronomy:

> The Scriptures say, "People do not live by bread alone, but by every word that comes from the mouth of God."
>
> —Matthew 4:4; Deuteronomy 8:3 NLT

> The Scriptures also say, "You must not test the LORD your God."
>
> —Matthew 4:7; Deuteronomy 6:16 NLT

> For the Scriptures say, "You must worship the LORD your God and serve only him."
>
> —Matthew 4:10; Deuteronomy 6:13 NLT

APPENDIX 2

You know how Satan tempted Adam and Eve by getting them to question God's truthfulness? He's still using that same old trick today. But here's the thing: When you truly know someone—I mean really know them—you don't fall for lies about their character.

The Bible isn't just another source of wisdom, it is truth. It is a comfort and a weapon against deception, especially lies about God's character. Just as he did with Adam and Eve, Satan is still trying to make you question whether God is truthful. But when you truly know God, you won't fall for lies about his character. This is why knowing God's Word is so important.

I am about to confess something to you. This is a secret I need to drag out into the light. I am a massive Dwayne "The Rock" Johnson fan. I'm serious! I don't exactly know why. A lot of his movies are cheesy, but I really enjoy them. Don't get me wrong, I don't believe he's a perfect role model. I may know all his movies (except for a few that are a little too explicit), and I may follow him on social media, and I may be able to tell you a bunch of facts about him. But I don't really know him, I just know about him. If I knocked on his door and said, "Hey, Rock!" he would be like, "Who are you? I don't know you." Even with all my knowledge about him, he would be right. I don't really know him, I only know about him, from a distance.

There's a difference between knowing about Jesus and

really knowing him. I don't want to just memorize information and verses about him. I want to know him so well I never question who he is and what he will do. Part of that comes from spending time with him in his Word.

That's exactly why knowing God's Word is crucial. If you're new to the Bible, let me help you get started. First, grab a translation you can easily understand—maybe the New Living Translation, New International Version, or English Standard Version. Begin with the Gospel of John and let that be your launching point. As you read, simply ask Jesus to help you understand what he's showing you. Make it a habit to spend time in his Word, and if you can, find someone who genuinely loves Jesus to read alongside you.

MATURE IN PRAYER

In today's world, we are conditioned to constantly be on—always with a phone, tablet, laptop, or some kind of screen in front of our faces. The idea of being unplugged and quiet enough to pray for more than a minute may seem daunting or flat out impossible. But prayer is a powerful tool for growing your faith because it demands faith. When you pray, you're relinquishing control and trusting God to do what you cannot.

When you pray, you're talking to Jesus. He is with you, and as with any relationship, you grow closer when you take time to speak and listen. Can you imagine being married and never speaking to your spouse or taking the time to listen to each other? You would grow apart and likely give your heart to someone else. It's the same with Jesus. When we act like he's not there by not communicating with him, we will begin to worship something else.

Jesus set the example for prioritizing prayer. When crowds of people were looking for him, he didn't run to the fame, he went off to be in prayer. "And rising very early in the morning, while it was still dark, he departed and went out to a desolate place, and there he prayed. And Simon and those who were with him searched for him, and they found him and said to him, 'Everyone is looking for you'" (Mark 1:35–37 ESV).

Like I said before, if Jesus did it, that's good enough for me. He is not the exception, he is the example.

Prayer doesn't have to be robotic, still, and formal. Just talk to him naturally, then take time to wait and quietly listen. If you hear something but are unsure whether it's his voice or your thoughts, check it against his Word, because he will never contradict himself. If what you're hearing doesn't line up with Scripture, it's not him. It's pretty simple: The more time you spend in God's Word and in prayer, the better you'll get at recognizing his voice and knowing him personally.

But no one is meant to be an island.

MATURE IN CHRISTIAN COMMUNITY

All this talk about personal prayer and Bible study might make you think you should just go off on your own, but you are not meant to go it alone. Of course you have Jesus, but you are made to be in fellowship with others. If you don't like people, then you're gonna hate heaven. I'm not saying you should stop being an introvert, but look at Jesus: He had twelve disciples and even brought some of them to pray with him. "He took with him Peter and John and James and went up on the mountain to pray" (Luke 9:28 ESV).

Jesus instilled in his disciples that believers should be together. You see this theme throughout the New Testament:

> For where two or three are gathered in my name, there am I among them.
>
> —Matthew 18:20 ESV

> My prayer is not for them alone. I pray also for those who will believe in me through their message, that all of them may be one, Father, just as you are in me and I am in you.
>
> —John 17:20–21

> All these with one accord were devoting themselves to

> prayer, together with the women and Mary the mother of Jesus, and his brothers.
>
> —Acts 1:14 ESV

> And let us consider how we may spur one another on toward love and good deeds, not giving up meeting together, as some are in the habit of doing, but encouraging one another.
>
> —Hebrews 10:24–25

There are many more examples like these. What I'm saying is find a church, Christian friends, or any gathering of believers who love Jesus and you. Spend time with them. Pray together. Encourage one another. Worship Jesus together. Read the Bible together.

You are not meant to be a lone ranger. The apostle Peter writes, "Watch out for your great enemy, the devil. He prowls around like a roaring lion, looking for someone to devour" (1 Peter 5:8 NLT).

Ever watched a nature show on which lions hunt? They always watch for the gazelle that strays from the herd. A prey animal is most vulnerable when isolated. The same is true when you try to go it alone in your faith. When you isolate yourself, depression, anxiety, and complacency find fertile ground in which to take root and flourish. Sometimes you need someone you trust to tell you that you're off about something or that you're not crazy. You need people who can encourage and lovingly correct you when needed. That's why it's crucial to find other believers to do life with. There are ways you will mature only when you're in community.

GIVE UP CONTROL

If we're honest, most of us will admit we want to be in control. If we've been let down a lot—hurt or disappointed enough times—it's scary to truly trust someone else, even God, for anything. We'd rather grab the controls ourselves and make things happen. That way we can't be let down.

You know that old saying, "Give a man a fish and you feed him for a day; teach a man to fish and you feed him for a lifetime"? I relate to it; it makes total sense to me. But here's a thought that challenges me: What if the person giving the fish is Jesus himself? Now, I'm not suggesting you should just sit around doing nothing. What I'm talking about is something deeper: trusting Jesus to be exactly who he says he is and taking him up on the incredible offer he made to you. "Come to me, all you who are weary and burdened, and I will give you rest. Take my yoke upon you and learn from me, for I am gentle and humble in heart, and you will find rest for your souls. For my yoke is easy and my burden is light" (Matt. 11:28–30).

You can let go of the anxiety of holding it all together and let God be the source of provision and control. It's okay. Scratch that! It's better than okay. I could dig the well myself, or I could come to the one who is living water. I could knead and bake my own bread, or be satisfied by the one who is the Bread of Life. Place it all where it belongs, in his hands.

Remember, none of this is about how you have to be like Jesus, it's that you *get* to be like him. You get to mature more and more into his likeness. I love you and I'm cheering you on. More important, Jesus is in you, cheering you on toward the goal, which is your being fully alive in him.

RESOURCES

ADDICTION RECOVERY MINISTRIES

Adult and Teen Challenge: https://teenchallengeusa.org

Celebrate Recovery: https://celebraterecovery.com

BIBLE STUDY TOOLS

Navigators: www.navigators.org/resource/bible-study-tools/

A good study Bible

BIBLE WEBSITES/APPS

YouVersion Bible: www.bible.com

Bible Gateway: www.biblegateway.com

Bible Memory App

PRAYER RESOURCES

Navigators: www.navigators.org/topic/prayer/

Echo Prayer App

Lectio 365 App

Pray As You Go App

BOOKS

The Case for Christ: A Journalist's Personal Investigation of the Evidence for Jesus, Lee Strobel

The Reason for God: Belief in an Age of Skepticism, Timothy Keller
Steps: A Guide to Transforming Your Life When Willpower Isn't Enough, John Ortberg
Why I Believe: A Psychologist's Thoughts on Suffering, Miracles, Science, and Faith, Henry Cloud

NOTES

CHAPTER 1: SON OF A PREACHER MAN

1. Matthew Brown, "Father's Faith: Perceptions of God May Stem from Dad-Child Relationships," *Washington Times*, June 15, 2013, www.washingtontimes.com/news/2013/jun/15/fathers-faith-perceptions-god-may-stem-dad-child-r/.

CHAPTER 4: DO-IT-AGAIN STORY

1. Marc Byrd and Steve Hindalong, "God of Wonders," New Spring Publications, 2000.

CHAPTER 5: FATHER, SON, AND BROKEN SPIRIT

1. Jason Clayborn and Stephen McWhirter, "Rapha," Integrity Music, 2022.

CHAPTER 6: SEVENTY TIMES SEVEN

1. "The Forgiveness Project," cited in Harold Vaughan, "The Curse of Unforgiveness: Three Major Consequences," Harrison House, October 2024, https://harrisonhouse.com/blog/harold-vaughan-the-curse-of-unforgiveness-3-major-consequences.
2. "Forgiveness: Your Health Depends on It," Johns Hopkins Medicine, n.d., www.hopkinsmedicine.org/health/wellness-and-prevention/forgiveness-your-health-depends-on-it.

CHAPTER 7: NEVER BEEN THIS WAY BEFORE

1. C. S. Lewis, *The Weight of Glory: And Other Addresses* (1949; San Francisco: HarperOne, 1980), 46.

CHAPTER 9: COME JESUS COME

1. Hank Bentley, Bryan Fowler, Stephen McWhirter, and Tara McWhirter, "Come Jesus Come," Essential Music Publishing, 2020.

CHAPTER 10: THE THRESHING FLOOR

1. Daniel Doss, Stephen McWhirter, and Jason Clayborn, "Threshing Floor," Integrity Music, 2023.

ABOUT THE AUTHOR

Stephen McWhirter is a Louisville, Kentucky, native. He and his wife, Tara, have been together for more than twenty-eight years. They have three boys: Andrew, Alex, and Austin. Stephen has been leading worship for more than twenty-three years, and ten of those years have been spent as a full-time songwriter, recording artist, and traveling worship leader, sharing his testimony and seeing many come to Christ. Stephen is passionately committed to worshiping Jesus and leading others to him. He is a songwriter and artist with Capitol Christian Music Group.

You can connect with Stephen, his music, and his ministry here:

WEBSITE: worshipjesus.life
CONTACT: worshipjesus.life/contact
YOUTUBE: @stephenmcwhirter or youtube.com/stephenmcwhirter
INSTAGRAM: @stephenmcwhirter or instagram.com/stephenmcwhirter
FACEBOOK: @stephenmcwhirtermusic or facebook.com/stephenmcwhirtermusic
TIKTOK: @stephenmcwhirtermusic
THREADS: @stephenmcwhirter

From the Publisher

GREAT BOOKS

ARE EVEN BETTER WHEN THEY'RE SHARED!

Help other readers find this one:

- Post a review at your favorite online bookseller
- Post a picture on a social media account and share why you enjoyed it
- Send a note to a friend who would also love it—or better yet, give them a copy

Thanks for reading!